Weekend Walks

in Brooklyn

Weekend Walks

in Brooklyn

22 Self-Guided Walking Tours
from Brooklyn Heights to Coney Island

Robert J. Regalbuto

The Countryman Press
Woodstock, Vermont

ISBN 978-0-88150-806-2

Cover photo © Lee Foster
Interior photos by the author unless otherwise specified
Cover design by Dede Cummings Design
Text design and composition by Chelsea Cloeter
Maps by Moore Creative Design, © The Countryman Press

Published by The Countryman Press,
P.O. Box 748, Woodstock, Vermont 05091

Distributed by W. W. Norton & Company, Inc.,
500 Fifth Avenue, New York, NY 10110

Manufactured in the United States of America

10 9 8 7 6 5 4 3 2 1

In fond memory of my aunts and uncles

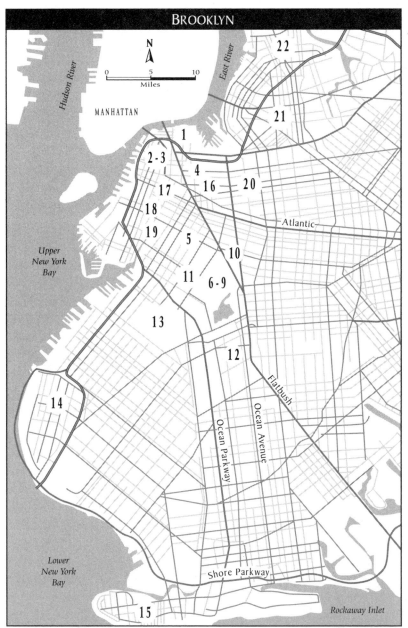

BROOKLYN

N

0   5   10
Miles

Hudson River

East River

MANHATTAN

1

2 - 3

4

16   20

17

18

19

5

Atlantic

10

11

6 - 9

Upper
New York
Bay

13

22

21

12

Flatbush

Ocean Avenue

Ocean Parkway

14

Lower
New York
Bay

Shore Parkway

15

Rockaway Inlet

© The Countryman Press

Contents

Weekend Walks in Brooklyn

Acknowledgments

I am happy to have this opportunity to say a word of thanks to my brother, Joseph F. Regalbuto Jr., for reviewing the manuscript and, beyond that, making valuable suggestions for additions to the book. I am grateful to Sarah Novak, Douglas Yeager, Lisa Sacks, and Kermit Hummel of The Countryman Press editorial staff for all their work on the manuscript. My thanks also to Dennis A. Walker and Phil Leeds for their help on the computer. So, too, I thank the following for supplying some of the photographs for this guide: Jesse Adelman of the Prospect Park Alliance, Richard Cox of the Harbor Defense Museum, Roxanne Robertson of the New York Transit Museum, Mara McGinnis of Pratt Institute, and Millie Perry of One Hanson Place.

Introduction

Brooklyn is full of surprises. Few realize that one in four Americans has roots in Brooklyn. Or that Brooklyn, if it were independent of New York City, would be the nation's fourth largest city, surpassing Philadelphia for that distinction. According to the 2000 census, Brooklyn, with a population of nearly 2,500,000, has more citizens than Boston, Atlanta, St. Louis, and San Francisco in total. It is New York City's most populous borough and, at about 80 square miles, its second largest in area.

But it is not size alone that distinguishes Brooklyn. To many it is a beloved place. Songs and poems have been penned about Brooklyn. And it has been the setting for novels, movies, TV shows, plays, and musicals. Beyond the historic, it is a part of American legend and lore. Hundreds of notable Americans were born in Brooklyn or have lived there. A partial list of artists and performers includes Woody Allen, Lauren Bacall, Mel Brooks, Eddie Cantor, Vic Damone, Tony Danza, Dom DeLuise, Neil Diamond, Richard Dreyfuss, Jimmy Durante, Lou Ferrigno, Jackie Gleason, Buddy Hackett, Susan Hayward, Rita Hayworth, Celeste Holm, Lena Horne, Harry Houdini, Danny Kaye, Alan King, Larry King, Julius La Rosa, Steve Lawrence, Spike Lee, Barry Manilow, Wynton and Branford Marsalis, Anne Meara, Robert Merrill, Alyssa Milano, Mary Tyler Moore, Zero Mostel, Eddie Murphy, Suzanne Pleshette, Martha Raye, Joan Rivers, Mickey Rooney, Neil Sedaka, Jerry Seinfeld, Beverly Sills, Phil Silvers, Paul Sorvino, Barbara Stanwyck, Connie Stevens, Barbra Streisand, Eli Wallach, Mae West, Shelly Winters, and Henny Youngman. Composers Aaron Copland and George Gershwin are from Brooklyn, as are writers and poets Isaac Asimov, Neil Simon, Norman Mailer, Arthur Miller, Walt Whitman, Marianne Moore, and Pete Hamill.

To the world of sports Brooklyn has contributed Michael Jordan, Jackie Robinson, Floyd Patterson, Sandy Koufax, Duke Snyder, Pee Wee Reese, Phil Rizzuto, Vince Lombardi, Joe Torre, Joe Pepitone, and commentator Howard Cosell, to name a few. Ruth Bader Ginsburg, associate justice of the U.S. Supreme Court, is from Brooklyn, as are former mayor Rudolph Giuliani, former governor Hugh Carey, and former congresswoman Shirley Chisholm.

The first people to inhabit what we now call Brooklyn were the Lenape Indians. They lived here year-round, sheltered in bark-covered long houses, each about 60 feet long and 15 feet wide. About eight families lived in a house, each gathering by its own fire for warmth and for cooking. They ate the vegetables they cultivated, the game they hunted, and the fish and shellfish they harvested from the shore. One spring day in 1524 Giovanni da Verrazano arrived in their waters, mooring his ship in the Narrows at a spot now overshadowed by the Verrazano-Narrows Bridge. The Lenape paddled their canoes to the ship and met these, the first Europeans to visit this area.

Eighty-five years later—in 1609—Henry Hudson followed, exploring the area for the Dutch. He navigated his ship the *Half Moon* through the Narrows and then up the river that would later bear his name. The Dutch began their colonization of "Nieuw Netherland" in 1624. "Breuckelen" was charted in 1646, named for a Dutch town from which many settlers came. Five more colonial settlements were established in the 1600s—all in today's borough. The British took over in 1664 and Breuckelen became anglicized variously to Brockland, Brocklin, Brookline, and Brooklyn. The English also named this Kings County in honor of King Charles II of England.

The Revolutionary War reached New York in 1776. The Battle of Brooklyn was fought in August. With the colonials led by George Washington, this was the first major land battle of the Revolution and a defeat for the Continental Army. What followed in Brooklyn was another great Revolutionary War tragedy: Wallabout Bay. Situated in the East River at the Navy Yard, the bay held British prison ships from 1776 to 1783. Through starvation, neglect, and disease, more than 11,000 American prisoners of war died on these ships.

The village of Brooklyn became a city in 1851. By the 1860s Brooklyn was America's third largest city. The Fulton Ferry strengthened ties with Manhattan, as did the opening of the Brooklyn Bridge in 1883. Thousands fled the congestion of Manhattan for Brooklyn, which in the 19th century was still largely rural and dotted with farms and estates. In 1898 Greater New York was formed and Brooklyn was no longer a city but a borough.

The Independent Rapid Transit subway line came to Brooklyn in 1908. The subways and els continued to spread throughout the borough. Wherever the trains went the building of apartment houses followed. For a time in the 1920s Brooklyn led the country in housing development. And Brooklyn's industries grew with its population. During World War II the Brooklyn Navy Yard employed 70,000 and it alone produced more ships than all of Japan.

This growing trend reversed after the war. Highways were built whisking former Brooklynites to Nassau and Suffolk Counties. Others moved to Staten Island after the completion of the Verrazano-Narrows Bridge in 1964. Many industries closed. The Navy Yard shut down in 1966. And a real morale deflator was the departure of the Dodgers for Los Angeles in 1957.

But Brooklyn's story does not end there. The Navy Yard has been privatized and is an industrial park with over 200 companies. In the late 1960s Brooklyn Heights was designated a national landmark and the city's first historic district. By the 1970s neighborhood associations began to take root. In South Brooklyn three distinct neighborhoods emerged, each claiming its own identity with historic and/or picturesque names: Carroll Gardens, Cobble Hill, and Boerum Hill. These and other neighborhoods such as Williamsburg and Greenpoint have been discovered by young professionals and families with children and are enjoying a period of growth and resurgence. Artists and other pioneers moved into the neighborhood of warehouses between the Brooklyn and Manhattan

Bridges. Now known as DUMBO ("down under the Manhattan Bridge overpass") this is one of the city's most upcoming and renewed districts. Starting in 1986, 16 acres in downtown Brooklyn were designated MetroTech Center. With an investment of over $300 million, MetroTech has attracted major corporations and created 25,000 new jobs. The newly built Atlantic Terminal and Center is a major transportation center, upscale shopping mall, and office building.

BAM (as the Brooklyn Academy of Music is now popularly known) has gained international recognition by hosting world-class performers and presenting avant-garde theater and cinema. The Brooklyn Museum has just completed a multimillion dollar expansion project that includes a dramatic entrance pavilion and plaza. Major restoration and conservation work continues at the Brooklyn Botanic Garden and at Prospect Park. There have been plans to bring the NBA Nets to Brooklyn, housing them in an arena to be designed by Frank Gehry whose Guggenheim Museum in Balboa, Spain, has received worldwide acclaim.

Brooklyn is rebounding, and there is a genuine interest in its history, heritage, notable persons, architecture, and sites. This book has been written as your guide as you explore Brooklyn by walking through its neighborhoods, down its many tree-lined streets past rows of Victorian brownstones, along the waterfront, and through its green spaces.

1 · DUMBO, Fulton Ferry, and Vinegar Hill

Directions: Take the 2 or 3 line to Clark Street subway station. Or take the A or C line to High Street. There is a water taxi from Manhattan (www.nywatertaxi.com). A walk over the Brooklyn Bridge will bring you to the start of this tour.

This walk encompasses three tiny neighborhoods: DUMBO, Fulton Ferry Landing, and Vinegar Hill. Many of us remember Dumbo the flying elephant in Disney's 1941 animated classic. Fewer know that DUMBO is today one of Brooklyn's most revitalized and upcoming neighborhoods. DUMBO is in fact an acronym for "down under the Manhattan Bridge overpass." This small area sandwiched between the Brooklyn and Manhattan Bridges was long referred to as the neighborhood "between the bridges." A cluster of warehouses, factories, and bars, these few blocks had little to recommend except for its great views of Manhattan. Things began to change in the 1970s when a few artist-pioneers from Manhattan bravely moved into warehouses. The colonization led to a population explosion in the 1990s and then full-blown gentrification. David Walentas now owns a lot of real estate in DUMBO and has been a driving force behind its development.

Flanking DUMBO are Fulton Ferry on the south and Vinegar Hill to the north. The early history of Brooklyn and that of Fulton Ferry Historic District are inseparable. In 1642 Dutch businessman Cornelis Dircksen began a small rowboat service linking "Breuckelen" with "Nieuw Amsterdam." A cluster of hotels, taverns, shops, and warehouses grew near "The Ferry." It was from this spot that George Washington and his men were spirited to Manhattan to escape the British after the Battle of Brooklyn

(1776). In 1814 Robert Fulton's steamboats began to replace the then prevalent horse-powered treadmill ferries, cutting the 90 minute cross-river trip down to a matter of minutes. "The Ferry" became known as "Fulton Ferry" and the neighborhood prospered. By the 1870s as many as 100,000 passengers were crossing the East River every day. One was Brooklynite Walt Whitman (1819–1892) who wrote in his poem "Crossing Brooklyn Ferry" from *Leaves of Grass*:

> *Flood-tide below me! I watch you face to face;*
> *Clouds of the west! Sun there half an hour high! I see you*
> *   also face to face....*
>
> *Others will enter the gates of the ferry, and cross from shore*
> *   to shore;*
> *Others will watch the run of the flood-tide;*
> *Others will see the shipping of Manhattan north and west,*
> *   and the heights of Brooklyn to the south and east;*
> *Others will see the islands large and small;*
> *Fifty years hence, others will see them as they cross, the sun*
> *   half an hour high;*
> *A hundred years hence, or even so many hundred years*
> *   hence, others will see them,*
> *Will enjoy the sunset, the pouring in of the flood-tide, the*
> *   falling back to the sea of the ebb-tide.*
>
> *It avails not, neither time or place—distance avails not;*
> *I am with you, you men and women of a generation, or*
> *   ever so many generations hence;*
> *I project myself—also I return—I am with you, and know*
> *   how it is.*

Fewer ferries crossed the river after the opening of the Brooklyn Bridge in 1883. The ferry became the slower, outmoded way to travel, and ferry service discontinued in 1924. Fulton Ferry was all but abandoned. The *WPA Guide to New York City* (published in 1939) describes the scene:

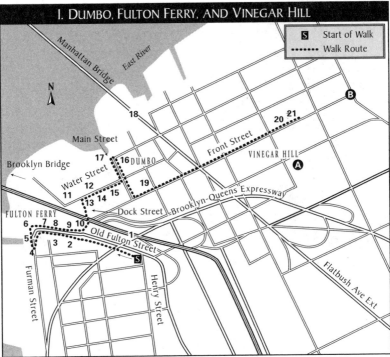

I. DUMBO, FULTON FERRY, AND VINEGAR HILL

S Start of Walk
••••••• Walk Route

© The Countryman Press

"Fulton Street, in this section, is now a sort of Brooklyn Bowery, with flop-houses, small shops, rancid restaurants, haunted by vagabonds and derelicts." Happily, like DUMBO, Fulton Ferry was "rediscovered" in the 1970s and is prospering again.

The third tiny district on this walk is Vinegar Hill. In the 1800s this enclave was also dubbed "Irishtown." It is named after Vinegar Hill in Wexford County, Ireland, where the Irish and the English battled in 1748. Many Vinegar Hill residents worked at the Navy Yard that abuts the neighborhood. The bars of Sands Street were frequented by the Navy Yard sailors who called it "Hell's Half Acre." The Navy Yard closed in 1966.

At the Clark Street subway station exit to Henry Street make a left on Henry Street and walk to the last street before the Brooklyn Bridge. This

CURRIER & IVES, 1881

THE BROOKLYN BRIDGE *An early view of the Brooklyn Bridge and Manhattan*

will be Old Fulton Street/Cadman Plaza West, which veers to the left and parallels the bridge. (Or, from the High Street subway station walk to Cadman Plaza West, which becomes Old Fulton Street, paralleling the bridge and leading you to the waterfront.)

The **Brooklyn Bridge (1)** was the first steel suspension bridge in the world. It is also a beautiful and legendary bridge. Thomas Wolfe, who lived in Brooklyn, in his book *Of Time and the River* writes about the bridge and its "wing-like sweep."

It took 14 years to build the bridge. John A. Roebling, an immigrant from Prussia, began work in 1869. Tragically, he died within weeks of starting the project and his son Washington Roebling took up his father's work. Despite many obstacles—including financial shortages, fires, and "the bends" suffered by Roebling and his men—the Brooklyn Bridge was completed in 1883.

Its length is 5,989 feet and its width is 85 feet. Each of the four cables is 15.75 inches wide and 3,578.5 feet long. The towers are 276.5 feet high above high water. When completed the bridge was the second tallest man-made structure in New York; only the spire of Trinity Church, Wall Street, was higher.

Over the last century and a quarter the Brooklyn Bridge has been crossed by carriages, cable cars, trolley cars, trains, bicycles, and automobiles. But a favorite and popular way to cross has been and remains by foot. The bridge's promenade is accessed on the Brooklyn side at Tillary Street and Adams Street/Brooklyn Bridge Boulevard—which is just one block east of Cadman Plaza East.

Continue your walk down Old Fulton Street/Cadman Plaza West, which you will see broadens considerably. The street was widened in 1855 and the left side then was covered with several sets of trolley tracks. When passengers arrived at Fulton Ferry many would board one of the horse-drawn trolleys that branched out through much of Brooklyn and the countryside beyond. Later, an elevated train line overshadowed the sidewalk you are walking on.

As you walk down Old Fulton Street on your left you will see a huge red brick, fortresslike building. Its entrance arch is clearly labeled: **Eagle Warehouse and Storage Company (2)**. Built in 1883 by architect Frank Freeman, for a century this was used for the storage of furniture, sterling silver, and other household items. In 1980 it was converted to condominiums.

Walk just a few steps further to 8 Fulton Street (at the corner). Built in 1861, this was the **Brooklyn City Railroad Company Building (3)**. This was the firm that operated the trolleys on the tracks that were nearby. Trolley tickets were sold here. The red brick Italianate building became apartments in 1975.

Cross the street to the Fulton Ferry Landing. **Bargemusic (4)** is on your left. This was a coffee barge used by the Erie Lackawanna Railroad. In 1977 violinist Olga Bloom had the barge towed here and imaginatively adapted it for use as a concert chamber. Several concerts are given weekly with a view of the Manhattan skyline for a backdrop (www.bargemusic .org; 718-624-2083).

The white building to the right of Bargemusic is the former **Fireboat**

House (5), which was built on the site of the Fulton Ferry Terminal (1865–1926). Fire hoses were hung to dry in its tower. No longer in use by Marine Company 7 of the New York City Fire Department, this is now the Brooklyn Ice Cream Factory, where your favorite flavors of ice cream are served—with great views! (718-246-3963).

Next on the right is **River Café (6)**. Another barge anchored here in 1977, it also offers superb views of Manhattan. Rather than chamber music, award-winning cuisine is offered here (www.rivercafe.com; 718-522-5200).

Cross Water Street to **Pete's (7)**, a restaurant operated by the Thristino family since 1894. Pete's is on the first floor of the former Franklin Hotel, which was built in 1835 (www.petesdowntown.com; 718-858-3510).

Walk up Fulton Street. On your left, at #19, is **Grimaldi's Pizzeria (8)**, another Fulton Ferry institution. The ovens at Grimaldi's are fueled with coal, and many will testify that the pizza here is one of the best in the city. The building, by the way, dates to 1748 (www.grimaldis.com; 718-858-4300).

Walk to the next corner: Fulton and Front Streets. Front Street used to "front" on the shoreline. What you see between here and the East River is landfill. One Front Street is the former **Long Island Safe Deposit Company Building (9).** The cast iron façade is an imitation of an Italian palazzo. The bank closed in 1891 and the building now houses a restaurant.

Take a step or two to **5-7 Front Street (10)**. This Greek Revival building dates to 1835. Once used by the Long Island Insurance Company, this is believed to be New York's oldest surviving office building. The first meeting to plan the Brooklyn Bridge assembled here.

Continue on Front Street to the next corner (Dock Street). Make a left on Dock Street and return to Water Street. On your left at 25-39 Water Street is the **Tobacco Inspection Warehouse (11)** (1860). To the right of that from 53 to 83 Water Street there is a long row of seven warehouses collectively known as the **Empire Stores (12)**. The architect was Thomas

A view of the Brooklyn Bridge from Old Fulton Street

Stone. The first set (on the left) was built in 1870; the rest date from 1885. The Empire Stores were used for the storage of raw materials: sugar, molasses, coffee beans, grain, etc. Many similar warehouses once lined Brooklyn's shores, earning it the nickname "the walled city."

Across the street from the Empire Stores (at 38 Water Street) is **St. Ann's Warehouse (13),** which states that it "has developed a world-wide reputation as one of New York City's rare European-style theaters. With its large, flexible open space, artists are free to stretch, both literally and imaginatively." The theater had its roots at Arts at St. Ann's in Brooklyn Heights (www.stannswarehouse.org; 718-834-8794).

Just next door at #56 is a former spice mill factory where you'll see the **Smack Mellon Studios (14).** For a sweet burst of energy drop in at **Jacques Torres Chocolates (15)** at 66 Water Street.

With your back to the Brooklyn Bridge walk down Water Street to Main Street. Make a left on Main Street and on your right will be the **Clock Tower Building (16)**. This sixteen-story factory was built in 1888 for Robert Gair who pioneered the manufacture of corrugated cardboard cartons. It is an early example of a concrete building. Little more than a century later David Walentas converted the factory to 124 luxury condominiums and galleries.

Walk to the end of Main Street and enter the parks: the **Empire–Fulton Ferry State Park (17)** on your left and the Brooklyn Bridge Park on your right. Rest your feet a bit and enjoy the views of the Brooklyn Bridge (left) and the Manhattan Bridge (right). A couple of movies were filmed in part in the Empire–Fulton Ferry State Park. One is the *Scent of a Woman* (1992) for which Al Pacino won an Academy Award. The other is the *King of New York* (1990).

A few words about the **Manhattan Bridge (18)**. It was built because the Brooklyn Bridge was a great success. The Brooklyn Bridge became overtaxed with traffic. To ease congestion, the Williamsburg Bridge was built in 1903 and the Manhattan Bridge in turn followed in 1910. Its first architect was Henry Hornbostel who proposed eyebars to support the roadway. His plan rejected, a suspension cable system (like that used on the Brooklyn Bridge) was accepted. Carrere and Hastings were hired as the new architects. Their best-known work, guarded by two proud lions, is the New York Public Library. The Manhattan Bridge has a span of 1,470 feet. You may walk across the bridge. Or you may enjoy its views while seated on the MTA B, D, N, or Q lines.

When you leave the parks at Main Street make a left on Front Street. The **Dumbo Arts Center/DAC (19)** will be on your left at 30 Washington Street.

Continue on Front Street. Walk "DUMBO"—that is "down under the Manhattan Bridge overpass" to Vinegar Hill.

Detour A: If you make a right on Bridge Street and walk one block to York Street you will see the Eskimo Pie Building (Bridge Street between York and Tillman). It was built in 1908 for the Thomas Meter Company. The ice cream treats came later. Note the glazed terra cotta façade!

On Front Street, just beyond Bridge Street, stop at #225-227 on your left. This is **Engine Company #7 (20)**, built in 1855. Today it is a private home.

Next is the former **Benjamin Moore Paint Factory (21)** at #231-233, built in 1908; William Tubby was the architect. Beyond the factory, also on your left, there is a row of early 19th-century Greek Revival townhouses.

Detour B: To see the former site of the Martyrs Tomb, walk on Front Street and make a right on Hudson Avenue. While there is little more to see than a vacant lot, the site is significant in that it was the burial place for 11,000 American soldiers. The men died as prisoners of war on 11 British ships anchored in Wallabout Bay in the East River. In 1805 their remains were reburied here and the "Martyrs Monument" marked the grave. Finally, in 1873 the remains were reinterred again, this time in a crypt below the Prison Ship Martyrs Monument at Fort Greene Park (see page 124).

2 · Brooklyn Heights I: The North Heights

Directions: Take the 2 or 3 line to the Clark Street subway station.

B rooklyn Heights is known as "New York's first suburb." Soon after the Fulton Ferry began its service to Manhattan in 1814, Brooklyn Heights farmers began to sell their land partitioned into 25-by-100-foot building lots. The area grew with fine homes, churches, and other institutions lining streets named for the original farming families.

After Brooklyn joined Greater New York in 1898 the Heights began a period of decline. The subway brought more residents in and many single-family homes were replaced with apartment houses and large hotels.

Composer Benjamin Britten lived in Brooklyn Heights, as did writers Truman Capote, Tennessee Williams, Thomas Wolfe, Norman Mailer, Henry Miller, and others. In 1965 Brooklyn Heights became the first New York City neighborhood to be designated a historic district. That propelled a period of resurgence that continues today.

Brooklyn Heights was the setting for the 1960s TV series "The Patty Duke Show." Some movies were filmed here that will be referenced during the walking tour.

When you exit the Clark Street subway station you will be on Henry Street, so named because in the 1830s Dr. Thomas W. Henry lived here. Make a right, cross Clark Street, and walk about a half block. The **First Presbyterian Church (1)** will be on your right (1846, William B. Olmstead, architect). The interior of this brownstone church has nine Tiffany stained glass windows. The memorial doorway was added in 1921.

Just across the street is the **German Evangelical Lutheran Zion**

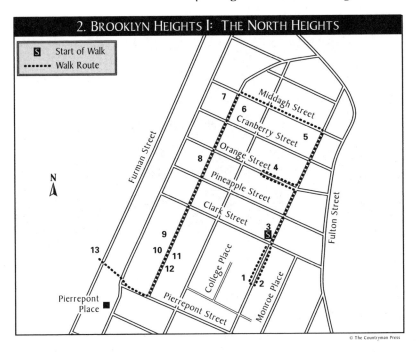

2. BROOKLYN HEIGHTS I: THE NORTH HEIGHTS

S Start of Walk
•••••• Walk Route

Church (2). When built in 1840, this was known as the Second Reform Dutch Church.

Retrace your steps and cross Clark Street again. William Clark made rope in his "ropewalk" nearby.

Note that the subway exit is on the ground floor of the former **St. George Hotel (3)**. The hotel was named for a tavern that stood here in the 1700s. The St. George opened in 1885 and by 1930 had grown to a complex of eight buildings. It was New York's largest hotel with 2,632 guest rooms, an Art Deco ballroom, and the world's largest indoor salt-water swimming pool. The St. George, as a hotel, no longer exists. A fire damaged the Clark Street side in 1995. What remains has been converted to condominiums and a gym.

Walk past the St. George on Henry Street. Continue for two short blocks, making note of the inviting eateries along the way.

Arthur Miller's house, 151 Willow Street, stop number 11 on this walk

Make a left on Orange Street. On your right is the **Plymouth Church of the Pilgrims (4)** (www.plymouthchurch.org; 718-624-4743). The great abolitionist Henry Ward Beecher was the minister at the Plymouth Church for forty years. (His sister was Harriet Beecher Stowe, who penned *Uncle Tom's Cabin*.) Beecher shared the pulpit with such luminaries as John Greenleaf Whittier, William Lloyd Garrison, and Charles Dickens. Abraham Lincoln worshiped here (see the plaque in pew 89) as did Mark Twain, Horace Greeley, Booker T. Washington, Clara Barton, and Dr. Martin Luther King, Jr.

A Congregational church, this was built in keeping with the austere style and spirit of New England meeting houses. The only addition to the outside of the church since Beecher's time is the entry porch.

The church seats a congregation of 2,800. A series of stained glass windows depicts the "History of Puritanism and its Influence Upon the Institutions and People of the Republic." These were made by Frederick Stymetz Lamb.

Just beyond the church is its garden, presided over by a statue of Henry Ward Beecher. The artist was Gutzon Borglum whose best known work is

Mount Rushmore. Beecher is admired here by a pensive Abraham Lincoln modeled in relief. The Plymouth Church (as this was first known) consolidated with the Church of the Pilgrims in 1934. The Tiffany stained glass windows from the Church of the Pilgrims may be seen here in Hillis Hall. (The former Church of the Pilgrims is now Our Lady of Lebanon Cathedral, which you'll see on the South Heights walking tour.)

Return to Henry Street and make a left. Make another left on Middah Street—named for property owner Aert Middah. Immediately on your left there is a 1929 **Firehouse (5)**. The mural on the door and the flowers and vigil candles are memorials to its firefighters who died on 9/11.

Middah Street has the most wooden houses in the Heights, and most of these date to the 1820s. Jog to the right on Hicks Street to see three restored 1830s houses (numbers 38, 38A, and 40).

Return to Middah Street. Make a right and stop at the **Eugene Boisselet House (6)** at #24 (corner of Willow Street). Built in the 1820s, this is an exquisite Federal period house.

The **Henry Ward Beecher House (7)** is at 22 Willow Street. This and the other Greek Revival houses in the row (20-26) were built about 1846.

Walk south on Willow Street. **Truman Capote's house (8)** is at #70. The author lived here in 1958 while writing *Breakfast at Tiffany's*. The Greek Revival house dates to 1839.

Continue your walk south on Willow Street past Pineapple and Clark Streets. On your right will be the **Dansk Somandskirke (Danish Seamen's Church) (9)** at #102.

Walk a few more steps to **numbers 108, 110, and 112 (10)** Willow Street. All three houses are the work of William Halsey Wood. Built in 1880, these are said to be the finest Queen Anne style houses in the city. Popular in the last quarter of the 19th century, Queen Anne houses usually featured steeply pitched roofs, large gables, bay windows, shingles, and Gothic and Renaissance decorative details.

Playwright **Arthur Miller's house (11)** is at 151 Willow Street. He lived here before marrying Marilyn Monroe. The house is a former carriage house dating to the 1880s.

Neighboring **numbers 155-159 (12)** Willow Street are red brick Federal houses dating to 1826. Note the glass pavement in front of #157, placed there to light a tunnel that was a part of the Underground Railroad.

Walk to Pierrepont Street, which was named for real estate developer Hezekiah Beers Pierrepont (1768–1838). Hezekiah's grandfather, Rev. James Pierrepont, founded Yale College in 1701. Make a right on Pierrepont and enter the **Esplanade (13)**. The Promenade (as it is also known) runs along the outer edge of the Heights, offering wonderful views of the Manhattan skyline, Upper New York Bay, and the Statue of Liberty. The Esplanade was cantilevered over the Brooklyn Queens Expressway in 1951.

Sit and enjoy the view. The second Brooklyn Heights walk in this book, exploring the South Heights, begins at this point. For a bite to eat remember the restaurants seen on Henry Street at the beginning of this tour. There are other places to eat on Montague Street, which is one block south of Pierrepont Street.

3 · Brooklyn Heights II: The South Heights

This walk begins where the first tour of Brooklyn Heights (the North Heights) ended.

After enjoying the views from the Promenade, exit at Pierrepont Street and make an immediate right onto Pierrepont Place. Note the twin houses on your right at **numbers 2 and 3 Pierrepont Place (1)**. These are said to be the handsomest brownstones in all of New York. Number 2 was the home of Alfred Treadway White, a fur trader and a philanthropist. White donated, among other things, the Japanese Garden at the Brooklyn Botanic Garden (see page 73). He also built low-rent housing for the poor as you will see later on this tour and also in the Cobble Hill tour (see page 135). Number 3 was built for Abiel Abbot Low. Low made his fortune in the China trade. His son Seth Low was the first mayor of Greater New York (after consolidation with Brooklyn in 1898) and the president of Columbia University. Both houses were built in 1857 and designed by Richard Upjohn (best known for his work on Trinity Church, Wall Street). A third house stood where there is a playground today. Part of the film *Prizzi's Honor* (1985) was filmed at #3.

Cross Montague Street to Montague Terrace. The Lady Mary Wortley Montagu (1689–1762) was a Pierrepont cousin. The **Thomas Wolfe House (2)** is at 5 Montague Terrace. Here he wrote *Of Time and the River*.

Retrace your steps and make a right onto Montague Street. **The Heights Casino (3)** is on your left at #75. It was built in 1905 by Boring and Tilton, who also designed the main buildings on Ellis Island. A private tennis and squash club, the casino is on the site of the 18th-century Pierrepont

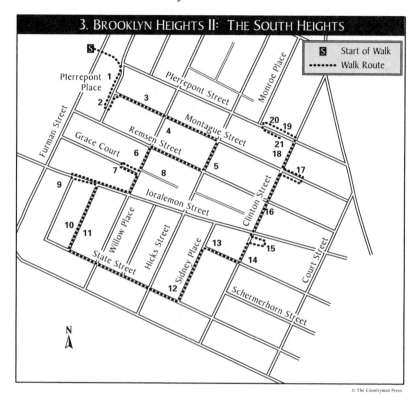

3. BROOKLYN HEIGHTS II: THE SOUTH HEIGHTS

S Start of Walk
••••••• Walk Route

Pierrepont Place
Furman Street
Pierrepont Street
Monroe Place
Montague Street
Grace Court
Remsen Street
Joralemon Street
Willow Place
Hicks Street
Sidney Place
Clinton Street
Court Street
State Street
Schermerhorn Street

N

© The Countryman Press

mansion named "Four Chimneys." George Washington made Four Chimneys his headquarters during the Battle of Brooklyn.

Continue your walk east on Montague Street. On your right, just beyond Hicks Street, is the former **Hotel Bossert (4)** (1908–1913, Helmle and Huberty, architects).

Walk to Henry Street and turn right. At the next corner, on your left, you'll see **Our Lady of Lebanon Cathedral (5)**. This was originally the Church of the Pilgrims (Congregational). It and the Plymouth Church consolidated at the Orange Street location in 1934. Built in 1844, this was the first Congregationalist church in Brooklyn and the first church of Romanesque style in America. Surprisingly, the architect was Richard

Upjohn whose forte was the Gothic Revival style. Note the south and west doors. These were salvaged from the luxury liner SS *Normandie*, which burned and sank in New York in 1942. The tower bell dates to 1864. Our Lady of Lebanon is a Roman Catholic Church. Its congregation is Lebanese and its services are conducted in the Maronite Rite (718-237-9913).

Make a right on Remsen Street and then a left on Hicks Street. **Grace Church (6)** (www.gracebrooklynheights.org; 718-624-1850) will be on your right. Walk down the garden path, past the 85-foot elm tree, and into the church. A Gothic masterpiece, this is another Richard Upjohn work. Upjohn was an Englishman who lived in Brooklyn (see page 133). Inside the sandstone church you'll see three Tiffany stained glass windows, an alabaster high altar, and an open wood vaulted ceiling. An Episcopal church, Grace has a choir of men and boys as do so many English Anglican parishes, cathedrals, and collegiate churches.

Visit **Grace Court (7)**, which parallels the nave of the church on its south side. Civil rights champion W. E. B. DuBois lived here, as did playwright Arthur Miller who wrote *Death of a Salesman*.

Across Hicks Street is **Grace Court Alley (8)** with its stables and carriage houses.

Walk south on Hicks Street to the corner and make a right onto the cobblestoned Joralemon Street. On your right there will be a row of 24 Greek Revival houses built in the 1840s. Number 58 is not a house but rather an emergency exit and ventilation for the MTA subway beneath. Walk on the bluestone sidewalk to Columbia Place (on your left). The **Riverside Apartments (9)** at 4-30 Columbia Place were built in 1890 by philanthopist Alfred T. White (whose house we saw earlier on this walk) as a "limited profit" housing project.

Retrace your steps on Joralemon Street and make a right on Willow Street. The **Willow Place Chapel (10)** is on your right at #26. Built as a mission of the First Unitarian Church in 1875, it now houses a nursery, music school, and theater. Russell Sturgis was the architect.

Across the street at **43-49 Willow Place (11)** there are four Greek Revival townhouses joined by a colonnade. These date to 1846.

At the end of Willow Street make a left onto State Street. Walk four short blocks to **103-107 State Street (12)** and note the exceptionally elegant cast iron balconies that date to 1848.

Make a left on Sidney Place. Ahead of you, on your right, is **St. Charles Borromeo Church (13)** (Roman Catholic). It is the work of Brooklyn-based Patrick C. Keely who designed hundreds of Gothic Revival churches and cathedrals.

Make a right on Aitken Place (named for a St. Charles pastor). And then make a left on Clinton Street. DeWitt Clinton (1769–1828) was a New York mayor and governor. In front of you, at the corner of Clinton and Livingston Streets, is the former **St. Ann's Church (14)**. It was designed in 1867 by James Renwick whose works include St. Patrick's Cathedral and the Smithsonian Castle. An outstanding example of High Victorian Gothic, its exterior has a "permanent polychrome" of dark brown and white stonework. St. Anne's was an Episcopal Church until 1966 when it merged with Holy Trinity Church. It is now a part of the Packer Collegiate Institute campus.

Walk north on Clinton Street one block to Joralemon Street. Make a right, and on your right you'll see **Packer Collegiate Institute (15)**, housed, fittingly, in the "Collegiate Gothic" Founders Hall (1854, Minard Lafever, architect). It is the successor to the Brooklyn Female Academy. The school was named for educator William S. Packer. Now coeducational, Packer is a private school for students from preschool through twelfth grade. The eight-building campus surrounds an award-winning, half-acre Alumnae Garden.

Walk north on Clinton Street. At the corner of Clinton and Remsen Streets (on your right) is the former **Spencer Memorial Church (16)** (Presbyterian). Built in 1850–1853, the church closed in 1970 and is now divided into condominiums.

Walk one more block to Montague Street. To your right you'll see a row of three architecturally distinctive **bank buildings (17)**. As bank names change often, I'll use their street addresses here. Closest to Clinton Street, 177 Montague Street is a copy of the Palazzo della Gran Guardia in

The former St. Ann's Church, stop number 14

Verona, Italy, designed by Domenico Curtoni in 1610. This limestone copy was built in 1910–1913 by York and Sawyer.

Next, at #183, is a 1903 Mowbray and Uffinger re-creation of an ancient Roman temple.

Finally, the third in the row of banks is dramatically different from the first two. The Art Deco building at 185 Montague Street is the 1930 work of Corbett, Harrison, and MacMurray. Following this they did work at Rockefeller Center.

Return to the corner of Montague and Clinton. Across the street from you is **St. Ann's and the Holy Trinity Church (18)** (Episcopal) (www.dioceselongisland.org/allparish/B16StAnnHolyTrinity.htm; 718-875-6960). This was originally Holy Trinity Church until it merged with St. Ann's in 1966. A Gothic Revival work, it was designed by Minard Lafever and completed in 1847. The exterior is brownstone and like most brownstone buildings it has weathered poorly. The church lost its lofty spire in 1905 because of subway construction.

In 1987 this church was declared a National Historic Landmark in recognition of its outstanding collection of stained glass windows. The sixty windows, crafted in the years 1844–1847, were the work of William Jay Bolton. The first American artist to create figural stained glass, Bolton was innovative in his use of vibrant colors. These windows depict chapters in the life of Christ, and their foretelling by Old Testament prophets. Many art historians agree that St. Ann's and the Holy Trinity contains what may be the finest single collection of stained glass windows in America.

After leaving the church make a left on Clinton Street. At the northwest corner of Clinton and Pierrepont Streets is **St. Ann's School (19)**. This was built as the Crescent Athletic Club in 1906; Frank Freeman was the architect. In 1940 the club closed and this was used as office space until 1966 when St. Ann's Church closed, merged with Holy Trinity, and bought the Crescent Club building for use as a school.

Just a few steps from the school is the **Church of the Saviour (20)**. This is the oldest Unitarian congregation in Brooklyn, founded in 1833. Eleven years later this church was built on the site of a 1780 British fort. Another Minard Lafever work, it was completed in 1844. The style is Gothic Revival and the building material is sandstone. In the 1890s the church was embellished with the addition of eight Tiffany stained glass windows.

Retrace your steps on Pierrepont Street to Clinton Street. On your right is the **Brooklyn Historical Society (BHS) (21)**. Founded in 1863 as the Long Island Historical Society, its name was changed in 1985. The society's building dates to 1878. George B. Post was the architect; he also designed the New York Stock Exchange building.

Before entering be sure to study the terra cotta artwork on the façade. This was the work of Olin Levi Warner. Warner studied at the Ecole des Beaux Arts in Paris. Over the main door there are depictions of the heads of an American Indian and a Viking. Other figures include representations of Christopher Columbus, Michelangelo, Benjamin Franklin, William Shakespeare, Ludwig van Beethoven, and Johann Gutenberg. Warner later produced artwork for the Library of Congress.

Enter the building and climb the grand staircase to view carved woodwork, stained glass windows, Minton floor tiles, and the Othmer Library. Opened in 1881, the library documents the history of Brooklyn with a collection of over 150,000 books, maps, and manuscripts, including the papers of the abolitionist and Brooklynite Henry Ward Beecher. The BHS's photo archive has more than 100,000 images and its museum collection has more than 9,000 objects. These include portraits and other artwork, Indian tools, and furnishings dating to the colonial era. In addition to the permanent collection, changing exhibits are mounted. The BHS offers tours, musical and other public programs, and educational opportunities (www.brooklynhistory.org; 718-222-4111).

This is where this tour ends. For a bite to eat walk one block south to Montague Street.

4 · Downtown

Directions: *Take the 2, 3, 4, or 5 line to Borough Hall. Or take the A, C, or F lines to Jay Street, Borough Hall.*

This area was a part of the Dutch village of Breuckelen when it was chartered in 1646. Soon after Brooklyn became a city in 1834, City Hall was built. This became Borough Hall when Brooklyn was swallowed into Greater New York City in 1898. Borough Hall was later surrounded by elevated railways. The area went through a major change in the 1950s when the "el" was taken down—as were many of the surrounding buildings, and today's Civic Center was developed. Downtown went through a period of decline starting in the 1960s. To reverse this trend, MetroTech Center was begun in 1986 to lure businesses to downtown Brooklyn. Downtown Brooklyn is New York City's third largest business district after Midtown Manhattan and Lower Manhattan.

Begin your tour at **Brooklyn Borough Hall (1)**. The outside is best seen from the north side (Cadman Plaza) where the flight of steps leads to a colonnade of six fluted Ionic columns. This was built 1836–1848 as Brooklyn's City Hall. The architect was Gamaliel King whose previous careers were that of a grocer and a carpenter. He used the Greek Revival style. The cupola above, however, is Georgian style. The original wooden cupola burned in 1895 and was soon replaced with the present cast iron duplicate. The exterior is faced with marble from Tuckahoe, New York. Borough Hall was restored in 1989. Tours are given on Tuesdays at 1:00 PM. To visit the Brooklyn Tourism Information Center enter Borough Hall at ground level at Joralemon Street (www.Brooklyn-usa.org; 718-802-3809).

At the Joralemon Street side of Borough Hall you will see two **IRT Subway Entrances (2)** which date to 1908. They were designed by Heins and

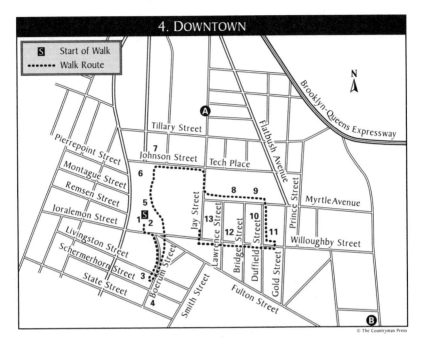

4. DOWNTOWN

S Start of Walk
•••••• Walk Route

N

Brooklyn-Queens Expressway

Tillary Street

A

Pierrepoint Street

Johnson Street

7

Tech Place

Flatbush Avenue

Montague Street

6

Remsen Street

5

Joralemon Street

8 **9**

Jay Street

Prince Street

Myrtle Avenue

1 S **2**

Livingston Street

13

Lawrence Street

12

Bridge Street

10

Duffield Street

11

Gold Street

Willoughby Street

Schermerhorn Street

3

Boerum Street

State Street

4

Smith Street

Fulton Street

© The Countryman Press

LaFarge. These are a lead-in to the next stop on your walk: the **New York Transit Museum (3)**. Cross Joralemon Street and make a right onto Boerum Place/Brooklyn Bridge Boulevard. Walk two blocks to Schermerhorn Street. At the corner of Schermerhorn and Boerum you will see an old subway entrance. Go down the steps. This is the entrance to the New York Transit Museum, which occupies a former subway station (www.mta.info/museum; 718-694-1600).

The largest museum of its kind in America, the 60,000-square-foot site has a collection of over 6,000 objects that run the gamut from 19 subway and el cars (some dating to 1904) to turnstiles, to tokens. And yes, you may board the trains and use the turnstiles. I found this a really fun museum that both adults and children enjoy. Special exhibits are mounted and programs offered such as excursions, lectures, screenings, and children's events. There are also a shop and an archive.

When you emerge from the museum look diagonally across the intersection to the red brick **Brooklyn Friends Meeting House (4)**. The meeting house, built for Quakers in 1857, is attributed to Charles T. Bunting.

Many of the streets in the area (including Joralemon and Schermerhorn) are named for early Dutch land owners.

Retrace your steps to Borough Hall. Walk around to the north side of Borough Hall to **Cadman Plaza (5)**. The plaza was created in the 1950s. It was named for Rev. Dr. Samuel Parkes Cadman (1864–1936) who was a Congregational minister based in Brooklyn. He gained nationwide attention through his radio broadcast sermons. The plaza is also named Columbus Park. Tents are set up here and the plaza is transformed into an ongoing farmer's market.

Walk north through the plaza. The New York State Supreme Court is on your right. Built in 1950, it is the work of Shreve, Lamb, and Harmon. They also designed the Empire State Building (1931).

The U.S. Eastern District Courthouse at 225 Cadman Plaza East has a gallery in which special exhibits are displayed.

Before you is a **statue of Henry Ward Beecher (6)**. Beecher (1813–1887) was the minister at Brooklyn's Plymouth Church and a leading abolitionist. The statue was modeled by John Quincy Adams Ward who is known as the "Dean of American Sculpture." When Beecher died on March 8, 1887, Ward rushed to his deathbed to make a death mask. It was used in creating this statue that has been hailed as an outstanding public monument. The black granite pedestal was designed by Richard Morris Hunt, often referred to as the "Dean of American Architecture."

Other monuments in Cadman Plaza honor Christopher Columbus (by Emma Stebbins in 1867) and Senator Robert F. Kennedy (by Anneta Duveen in 1972).

In back of the Beecher memorial, just across Johnson Street, is the **United States Post Office and Courthouse (7)**. A massive Romanesque Revival building, it is faced with granite, both rough and polished, and its towers, dormers, and roof are covered with slate. The south side of the building (facing the plaza) was completed in 1891 as designed by Mif-

ROBERT I. REGALBUTO

Brooklyn Borough Hall, stop number 1

Early wooden Brooklyn "el" car at the New York Transit Museum, stop number 3

flin E. Bell and William A. Freret. James Wetmore is responsible for the addition on the north side (1933).

Make a right on Johnson Street and walk to Jay Street.

Detour A: To visit the Cathedral Basilica of St. James, make a left on Jay Street and walk north two blocks. Founded in 1822, St. James was the first Roman Catholic church on Long Island. The present Georgian style building dates to 1903 (George H. Streeton, architect). For many years St. James was a procathedral (or temporary cathedral) pending the building of a permanent cathedral (on the BAM tour, see page 126). Since the cathedral was never completed, St. James was elevated to cathedral status in 1972. Pope John Paul II stopped here on October 3, 1979. An official decree from the Vatican dated May 6, 1982, bestowed the title of "The Cathedral-Basilica of St. James."

John Jay was a delegate to the 1st and 2nd Continental Congresses, author of five Federalist Papers, governor of New York, and the first chief justice of the U.S. Supreme Court. Walk south on Jay Street to Myrtle Avenue, so called because of the abundance of myrtle bushes that grew here. Make a left on Myrtle Avenue and walk to the park that is named **MetroTech Commons (8)**. You are at the heart of MetroTech Center, a revitalized neighborhood that covers 16 acres and includes 12 buildings. The project began in 1986 and was sponsored by the city of New York and Polytechnic University. MetroTech has attracted major corporations and created 25,000 new jobs.

MetroTech Commons is a 3.5-acre park with contemporary art, and a popular spot for lunchtime concerts and special events.

On the east side of the Commons you'll see the **Polytechnic Landmark Student Center (9)**. The 1847 Greek Revival building was originally the first Free Congregational Church. In 1854 the church was bought by Brooklyn's oldest black congregation (founded in 1818) and renamed the Brooklyn African Wesleyan Methodist Episcopal Church. It also became a stop on the Underground Railroad. In 1938 the congregation moved to Bedford-Stuyvesant. For a time the building was used as a factory. Restored in the 1990s, it is now Wunsch Hall, a student center for Polytechnic University.

Walk on Myrtle Avenue one more block and make a right on **Duffield Street (10)**. Note the early 19th-century houses on your right that were moved here and restored as a part of the MetroTech project. St. Boniface Church, also on your right, was founded by German immigrants in 1854. Designed by Patrick Keely, this church was built in 1872.

Duffield street intersects with Willoughby Street. The heiress Margaretta Duffield married the English émigré Samuel Willoughby in 1834. They owned the property here.

Walk to Willoughby Street and make a left. On your left will be the entrance to **4 MetroTech Center (11)**. Enter the lobby to see some high-tech art: the Chase Video Matrix (1992). It is the art of Nam June Paik, an American artist born in Seoul, Korea, in 1932. The mixed media work is a wall of 429 cable televisions, computers, and laser discs and may also be seen—in reflection—on the opposite wall.

From the door of 4 MetroTech Center make a right on Willoughby Street. Stop at the corner of Lawrence Street. The **New York and New**

Jersey Telephone Company building (12) is at 81 Willoughby. On the façade note the "TC" (for telephone company) over the doors as well as embellishments such as wall telephones, telephone receivers, and telephone bells. Built in 1898, this Renaissance Revival/Beaux Arts office building was designed by R. L. Daus.

Continue on Willoughby and make a right on Jay Street. On your right, at 365-367 Jay Street, is the **City of Brooklyn Fire Headquarters (13)**. Built in 1892, this Romanesque Revival firehouse was heavily influenced by the work of Henry Hobson Richardson. The architect was Frank Freeman. The building materials he used were sandstone, brick, and granite, and the roof is covered with tiles. The tower was a lookout for fires, and the broad arch was big enough for horse-drawn fire engines to pass through. Today this is an apartment building.

This is the end of your tour of downtown. To return to the starting point, walk to the end of Willoughby Street; Borough Hall will be in front of you.

Detour B: Junior's Restaurant, a Brooklyn institution, is about four blocks from the firehouse. It is at 386 Flatbush Avenue Extension (at the corner of DeKalb Avenue). Junior's founder was Harry Rosen. In 1929 he opened a nightclub on this site. Then in 1950 he closed the nightclub and opened a family-style restaurant, naming it "Junior's" in reference to his two sons. Though a full and varied menu is served, Junior's is best known for "the world's most fabulous cheesecake" (www.juniorscheesecake.com; 718-852-5257).

5 · Park Slope

Directions: *Take the 2 or 3 line to Grand Army Plaza.*

P ark Slope is so named because it is set on Prospect Hill, which descends from Prospect Park west to the Gowanus Canal. In the 1600s the Dutch bought this land from the Indian sachem Gouwane. It remained rural and undeveloped until the mid-1800s when real estate developer Edwin C. Litchfield bought the farms here and divided them into lots. His estate (at Prospect Park West and Fifth Street) became a part of Prospect Park (see pages 83–85). The opening of the Brooklyn Bridge in 1883 made a commute to Brooklyn relatively short. Many New York professionals built their mansions here and Park Slope became known as the "Gold Coast of Brooklyn." The Slope went through a period of decline in the mid-20th century. By the 1970s Park Slope was rediscovered and "gentrified." It has become, once again, one of the most attractive and desirable neighborhoods in the city.

From the subway station walk down Plaza Street West a short distance and make a right on Lincoln Place. On your right you'll see what resembles an Italian Gothic palazzo or, more specifically, the 15th-century Ca d'Oro ("House of Gold") built on Venice's Grand Canal. Here we have not a palace but rather a private club: the **Montauk Club (1)**. When built in 1891 (Francis H. Kimball, architect) this was a highly exclusive men's enclave. Women guests were admitted through a secondary door. This side door is no longer in use, and the club's membership is now more inclusive. Be sure to take a close look at the brownstone and brick façade. A terra cotta frieze wraps around the club on which are depicted Montauk Indians. Another terra cotta relief above the main door on Eighth Avenue shows the club's forefathers laying this building's cornerstone. Note also

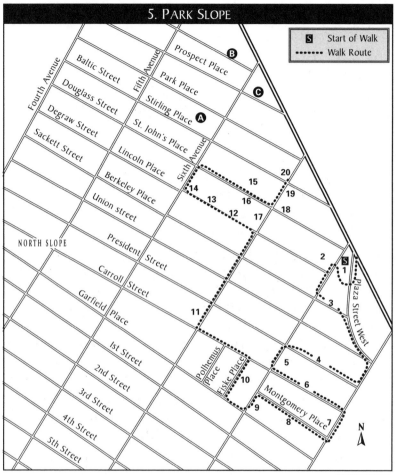

5. PARK SLOPE

S Start of Walk
••••••• Walk Route

Fourth Avenue
Baltic Street
Fifth Avenue
Prospect Place **B**
Douglass Street
Park Place **C**
Degraw Street
Stirling Place
Sackett Street
St. John's Place **A**
Lincoln Place
Sixth Avenue
Berkeley Place
Union street
NORTH SLOPE
President Street
Carroll Street
Garfield Place
1st Street
2nd Street
3rd Street
4th Street
5th Street
Polhemus Place
Fiske Place
Montgomery Place
Plaza Street West

14 13 12 15 16 17 20 19 18
2 1 3 11 5 4 10 6 9 8 7

N

© The Countryman Press

the Indian faces on the capitals and the wrought iron fence. The club's interior (five floors) no longer includes the bowling alley in the basement or the guest rooms on the top two floors. These have been sold for use as condominiums. The club, however, has kept the best of the interior: the first and second floors decorated with richly carved mahogany, Venetian Gothic arches, mosaics, and stained glass windows. Notable guests at the club have included four presidents: Grover Cleveland, Herbert Hoover, Dwight Eisenhower, and John Kennedy.

Across the street, **22 Eighth Avenue (2)** was the brownstone home of William J. Gaynor, one-time mayor of Greater New York. After taking office in 1910 he made it his habit to walk from his home to the Brooklyn Bridge, across the bridge, and then to his office at City Hall. That was a 4-mile walk! In 1910 Gaynor was shot in the throat by a man who had been fired from his municipal job. Gaynor survived the shot and resumed his walks. In 1913 Mayor Gaynor opened and dedicated Ebbets Field, home of the Brooklyn Dodgers baseball team. He died shortly thereafter.

Walk south on Eighth Avenue and make a left on Berkeley Place. (George Berkeley was an 18th-century Anglican bishop, philosopher, and scholar.) Stop at **276 Berkeley Place (3)**, which was the home of George P. Tangeman who made his fortune in the Royal and Cleveland Baking Powder companies. His granite, brick, and terra cotta Romanesque Revival house was built in 1891; Lamb and Rich were the architects.

Make a right onto Plaza Street West. Cross Union Street and walk one block to President Street. Make a right on **President Street (4)**. Walk one block to Eighth Avenue. The row houses on President Street date from the 1870s through the 1890s.

Make a left on Eighth Avenue and on your left (at #105) you will see a lovely Regency Revival house with a bowed limestone façade. This is now the **Montessori School (5)**. It was built in 1916. Frank J. Helmle was the architect. He also designed Prospect Park's Boathouse and Tennis Pavilion.

Walk a few more steps to the twin houses at **115 and 119 Eighth Avenue**. They were built in 1888 for Thomas Adams Jr. and his son. Adams invented Chiclets chewing gum and then to sell his gum he invented the automatic vending machine to dispense it. The architect C.P.H. Gilbert employed a Romanesque Revival style inspired by the work of Henry Hobson Richardson.

Cross Carroll Street. **Number 123 Eighth Avenue** is an 1894 Italian Renaissance design by Montrose W. Morris. Note the decorative tympanum over the door and the classical columns and pilasters framing the windows.

Walk east and stop at **838 Carroll Street (6)** on your right. It was built for James W. Remington in 1881, then president of the United States Law Association. The architect for this and the next two houses was C.P.H. Gilbert. These brownstone and brick mansions are some of the best Romanesque Revival houses in America.

Continue on Carroll Street. The houses on this block date to the 1880s and 1890s. The variety and styles and building materials make this block a textbook of late 19th-century architecture. Some examples: on your right #848 is neoclassical, numbers 858-856 are crafted of orange Roman brick, #860 is a Romantic design, #862 has a façade of polychrome sandstone and brick, numbers 870-872 combine the Shingle and Queen Anne styles, and #876 is a Georgian brick and limestone house.

Across the street note the row of Romanesque Revival houses numbered 855-861. Designed by Stanley M. Holden, the façades are yellow Roman brick trimmed with brownstone.

Make a right onto Prospect Park West. **Numbers 18 and 19 Prospect Park West (7)**, designed by Montrose W. Morris and built in 1898, are Renaissance Revival houses with limestone façades. Note the rusticated ground floor and the Palladian window—in imitation of the work of the 16th-century Italian architect Andrea Palladio.

Make a right at the next corner and walk down **Montgomery Place (8)**. General Richard Montgomery (1736–1775) led Continental troops during the Quebec campaign. Killed in battle, he is buried at St. Paul's Chapel near City Hall.

Many say that Montgomery Place is Park Slope's most beautiful street. Architectural historians consider it one of the most significant blocks of urban row houses. It was planned by real estate developer Harvey Murdock, who lived at #11. Of the 46 houses on the block, 20 are the work of C.P.H. Gilbert.

At the corner of Montgomery and Eighth Avenue, make a left. At the next corner, on your left, is the **Congregation Beth Elohim (9)** ("House of God"), the work of Simon Eisendrath and B. Horowitz. Garfield Temple, as it is often called, is a limestone Beaux Arts building crowned with a dome. The temple's entrance door is at an angle at the corner of the lot. The result is a five-sided temple, which may be a reference to the Pentateuch or Five Books of Moses (www.congregationbethelohim.org; 718-768-3814).

Make a right onto Garfield Place (that is, walking away from the park). This street was named in memory of President James Garfield, assassinated in 1881. Walk one short block on Garfield Place and make a right onto **Fiske Place (10)**. The row houses at 12-16 were built in 1896. Note the three bay windows: the first a triangle, the second a semicircle, and the third a square.

At the end of Fiske Place make a left on Carroll Street. Charles Carroll of Maryland was the only Roman Catholic to sign the Declaration of Independence. His Brooklyn connection is that he was instrumental in sending troops from Maryland to fight in the 1776 Battle of Brooklyn. Walk on Carroll Street to Seventh Avenue. The **Old First Reformed Church (11)** is before you. This Dutch Reformed congregation first gathered in 1656 and their first church was built ten years later on what became Fulton Street. This granite and limestone Gothic Revival church is the fourth to serve the congregation. It was built in 1893, designed by George L. Morse, architect.

Make a right and walk north of Seventh Avenue. If you're hungry at this point you'll see there are a number of restaurants along this stretch of Seventh.

Make a left on Lincoln Place. Stop at the **Frank L. Babbott House (12)** at #153. Mrs. Babbott was a Pratt whose father made a fortune in the Standard Oil Company and founded Pratt Institute (see Chapter 20 of this guide). Lamb and Rich designed this house in 1887.

The **John Condon House (13)** is at 139 Lincoln Place. Condon was a florist whose greenhouse was opposite the main gate of the Green-Wood Cemetery.

Walk a few more steps to the corner of Sixth Avenue. On your right is

Carroll Street between Prospect Park West and Eighth Avenue

the **Sixth Avenue Baptist Church (14).** This is a charming little church erected in 1880. Lawrence B. Valk was the architect. Unfortunately the church lost its steeple in the hurricane of 1938.

Make a right on Sixth Avenue. Walk one block and make another right on St. John's Place. You'll see the street's namesake on your left: **St. John's Episcopal Church (15).** Built in 1869, this is Park Slope's oldest church. The church, chapel, rectory, and garden form a picturesque enclave you'd expect to find in an English village.

Opposite the church are **176 and 178 St. John's Place (16).** These twin houses were built in 1888 for two physicians: Dr. Edward Bunker and Dr. William M. Thallon. If you look closely at the gable over the door at #178 you will see the caduceus (two snakes on a staff with wings above, symbolizing the medical profession). R.L. Daus was the architect and he let his imagination (and talent!) run wild here, embellishing the brick and brownstone Queen Anne houses with arches, dormers, gables, finials, and a tower with Gothic and Romanesque details.

Walk to the corner of Seventh Avenue. On your right is **Memorial Presbyterian Church (17)**. Dating to 1882, the church is constructed of Belleville, New Jersey, sandstone and topped with an octagonal spire. Pugin and Walter were the architects.

Diagonally across the intersection there's another Protestant church: **Grace United Methodist Church (18)** (1882, Parfitt brothers, architects). Grace also lost its spire to a hurricane (1944). At this point in your walk it will be obvious why Brooklyn earned the title City of Churches!

Next to Grace Church, at 21 Seventh Avenue, is the **Lillian Ward House (19)**. Miss Ward was an opera singer. Her house was built in 1887 by Lawrence B. Valk.

This intersection—Seventh Avenue and Sterling Place—was the **site of a plane crash (20)** on the foggy morning of December 16, 1960. Two planes, a TWA Constellation and a United Airlines DC-8, collided in midair. The TWA constellation crashed onto a Staten Island airfield. The DC-8 headed for Prospect Park for a landing but fell short of its target by just two blocks, landing here. The plane's nose rested on the front doorstep of the Ward mansion. All 84 on board were killed. The Pillar of Fire Church and a funeral home went up in flames and were lost. For decades the lots on the west side of Seventh Avenue were empty reminders of the tragedy. Then condominiums were built on the southwest corner. At the time of writing a building is under construction at the northwest corner.

This is where your tour of Park Slope ends. The nearest subway station is just one block north at Flatbush Avenue. This is the Seventh Avenue station on the Q and B lines.

Detour A: Having seen a temple and several Protestant churches on this walk, it is only fair (or at least bipartisan or ecumenical) to see a Roman Catholic church of note. St. Augustine's Church stands at 116 Sixth Avenue between Sterling Place and Park Place. It is the work of the Parfitt Brothers, Englishmen transplanted to Brooklyn. Dating to 1888, this is thought to be one of Brooklyn's best church buildings. More a Victorian Gothic cathedral than a church, its interior is fitted with beautifully carved marble statuary and large, exceptionally fine Tiffany stained glass windows.

Detour B: And now for something completely different. Number 182 Sixth Avenue has a remarkably well-preserved 19th-century storefront. It stands at the corner of St. Mark's Place.

Detour C: Also at the corner of Sixth Avenue and St. Mark's Place is the Cathedral Club of Brooklyn (at 85 Sixth Avenue). Built as a clubhouse in 1890, it housed the Carlton Club, then the Monroe Club, and later the Royal Arcanum Club. Finally in 1907 this became the Cathedral Club thanks to the efforts of Fr. George Mundelein who later became the Cardinal Archbishop of Chicago.

6 · Prospect Park I:
The Plaza and the Long Meadow

Directions: Take the 2 or 3 line to Grand Army Plaza.

P rospect Park (www.prospect park.org; 718-965-8999) was the vision of Brooklyn civic leader James Stranahan. Inspired by Central Park, he and Egbert Viele (who had been Central Park's chief engineer) came up with a site for the park that included what was then farmland on both sides of Flatbush Avenue. That was in 1859. The park's development was put on hold during the Civil War. The architect Calvert Vaux was brought in. On his recommendation the park's site was moved entirely west of Flatbush Avenue. Vaux and the landscape architect Frederick Law Olmsted created the 560-acre Prospect Park between 1866 and 1873. This included the acquisition of the estate of Edwin C. Litchfield whose mansion is the park's administrative center.

At the end of the 19th century the firm of McKim, Mead, and White made dramatic changes to the park's borders, replacing the original rustic wood fences with stone walls and adding the triumphal entrances we know today.

Robert Moses was appointed New York City's Parks Commissioner in 1934. He added Prospect Park's zoo, the bandshell, and several playgrounds. He saw the park as a place of recreation, which was at odds with the vision of Olmsted and Vaux who had created Prospect Park as a place of pastoral experience and as an escape from crowded urban life.

By the late 1960s time, neglect, deterioration, vandalism, and crime had taken its toll and the park's annual visitation was at an all-time low of 1.7 million visitors. The Prospect Park Alliance in partnership with

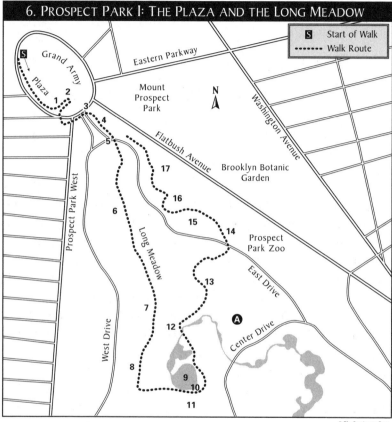

6. PROSPECT PARK I: THE PLAZA AND THE LONG MEADOW

S Start of Walk
•••••• Walk Route

Grand Army Plaza

Eastern Parkway

Mount Prospect Park

N

Washington Avenue

Flatbush Avenue

Brooklyn Botanic Garden

Prospect Park West

Long Meadow

Prospect Park Zoo

East Drive

West Drive

Center Drive

© The Countryman Press

Prospect Park administrator Tupper Thomas have reversed that trend. The park's ecosystem has been restored, as have many of its bridges, monuments, and rustic shelters. Crime in the park dropped significantly. Now about 6 million people enjoy Prospect Park each year.

From the Grand Army Plaza subway station walk south along Plaza Street West. Note the "berms" (mounds of earth) on your left, thoughtfully placed there to buffer this residential street from the buzz of traffic encircling the plaza. When you reach Union Street cross Plaza Street West. You'll be at the **statue of Gouverneur Kemble Warren (1)**. This was sculpted by Henry Baerer in 1896. Warren was a hero at the Battle of Gettysburg and stones from Gettysburg are a part of the monument's pedestal.

But on to bigger things. Before you is **Grand Army Plaza (2)**, an 11-acre oval plaza and the main entrance to Prospect Park. At first this was known as Prospect Park Plaza. It did not always look this way. Early on it had a fountain spurting a single jet of water. Dissatisfied with such a lackluster approach to the park, Brooklyn Mayor Seth Low proposed that a Civil War soldiers and sailors memorial replace the fountain. A competition was held and the winning design was that by John H. Duncan. Duncan later went on to design Grant's Tomb. But here the memorial was inspired by the Arc de Triomphe at the Place de l'Etoile in Paris. It is granite and stands square at 80 feet high and 80 feet wide. The arch is 50 feet high. Civil War General William Tecumseh Sherman laid the cornerstone in 1889; President Grover Cleveland dedicated the arch in 1892.

At first the monument stood without statuary. In 1894 artist Frederick MacMonnies was commissioned to model three groups of sculpture for the arch. The year before he sculpted the much admired statue "Columbia Enthroned" for the Columbian Exposition in Chicago. Look at the arch. On your left is the sculpture group entitled "The Spirit of the Army." "The Spirit of the Navy" is on your right. On top of the arch stands the "Quadriga," depicting the Lady Columbia (representing the victorious Union) riding a triumphal chariot pulled by a team of four horses. The horses are led and heralded by trumpet-blowing winged angels. The three sculpture groups were set in place between 1898 and 1901. In 1976 Columbia was almost blown away in a windstorm. Resecured, it and the other sculptures have since been restored.

To get a closer look at the arch cross the plaza near Union Street. Be mindful of the crosswalks and lights. On closer inspection, within the arch you will see two relief sculptures. One is the only known depiction of Abraham Lincoln on horseback. Opposite Lincoln is Ulysses S. Grant. The famous Philadelphia artist Thomas Eakins modeled the horses; William Rudolf O'Donovan sculpted the men.

The inside of the arch is sometimes open to the public who may climb the stairs to the top and enjoy the views. Art exhibits are occasionally mounted inside, too. For more information call 718-965-8999.

As you look through the arch you will see the Mary Louise Bailey Fountain (1932). It was a gift of Brooklyn philanthropist Frank Bailey as a memorial to his wife. He chose Edgerton Swarthout as architect and Eugene Francis Savage as sculptor. The central standing figures are Wisdom and Felicity.

Beyond the fountain there is a bust of President John F. Kennedy modeled by Neil Estern in 1965.

Return to Union Street. From there cross Prospect Park West to the park **entrance (3)**. Stanford White designed the granite pavilions, the urns, and the four Doric columns, each 35 feet high and crowned with bronze eagles.

A special note: every Saturday in season there is a "GreenMarket" (or farmers' market) held in tents here. The vendors sell their vegetables, fruits, and other foods from 8 AM to 4 PM.

Cross the driveway and enter the park just before the eagle column at the corner of Flatbush Avenue. As you enter note the **statue of James Stranahan (4)**, also sculpted by Frederick MacMonnies, and be sure to say "thank you" for making Prospect Park possible.

Walk a few more steps and you'll approach the **Endale Arch (5).** The name is an abbreviation "enter the dale." Brick and sandstone, the passage through the arch was originally covered with wood. Olmsted and Vaux planned this, a dramatic approach to one of Prospect Park's gems: the **Long Meadow (6)**.

After walking through the arch begin to walk the length of the meadow. Along the way, on your right, you will see a red brick building. This is the **Picnic House (7)**. Built in 1926, it replaced an earlier, more rustic one. It may be rented for private parties. Restroom facilities are here.

Continue along the open field. Next on your right you'll see what is my favorite building in Prospect Park: the **Tennis Pavilion (8)**. It's my favorite because it was one of my hangouts when I was a youngster. Aside

Grand Army Plaza, stop number 2

from that, it is a beautiful building. Walk inside and see if you agree. This Renaissance Revival pavilion was inspired by the work of the 16th-century Italian architect Andrea Palladio. This was built in 1910, designed by Helmle, Huberty, and Hudswell, architects. At that time lawn tennis was a popular pastime and the basement here was storage space for nets, etc. Restored in the 1970s and 1980s, the Tennis Pavilion is now head-quarters for the Brooklyn Center for the Urban Environment (BCUE) (www.bcue.org; 718-788-8549). The BCUE seeks to educate the public about the natural environment through walking tours and programs for school groups.

On both sides of the Tennis Pavilion there are paths that will lead you across the Long Meadow, past the **Upper Pool (9)**, and on to Fallkill. ("Kill" is the Dutch word for "waterway.") Walk over the **Fallkill Bridge (10)**. The **Fallkill Pond and Falls (11)** will be on your right. After the bridge take the first fork on your left, which will lead you over the rustic **Esdale Bridge (12)**.

Detour A: If you wish to explore the nature paths through the wooded area, turn right after crossing the Esdale Bridge. This will lead you to "Midwood."

After the Esdale Bridge bear right and circle **Sullivan Hill (13)**. This is named for the American General John Sullivan who was captured here by the British during the Battle of Brooklyn (1776).

At Battle Pass follow the path and cross East Drive. The **Dongan Oak Monument (14)** marks the site of a large white oak tree. In 1685 the English Colonial Governor Thomas Dongan settled a dispute by mandating this spot as the borderline between Brooklyn and Flatbush, marking it with a white oak. Ninety years later the tree was chopped down to block the advancing British troops. Look for this, a four-sided granite column with a bronze eagle perched on top. A plaque on the plinth recounts the events of the Battle of Brooklyn.

From the monument walk north and **Nellie's Lawn (15)** will be on your left. Nellie was a little girl who was often seen sitting under an elm tree here and reading—hence the name.

Continue north to the **Vale of Cashmere (16)**. The vale is a pond visited by birds and surrounded by lush greenery. The name was inspired by Thomas Moore's 1817 poem "Lalla Rookh":

> *Who has not heard of the Vale of Cashmere,*
> *With its roses the brightest*
> *The earth ever gave.*
> *Its temples and grottoes, and*
> *Fountains as clear*
> *As the love-lighted eyes that*
> *Hang over their wave.*

And a **Rose Garden (17)** does in fact border the vale on its eastern side.

This is where your tour ends. Walk north to return to Grand Army Plaza.

7 · Prospect Park II: Willink Corner and the Zoo

Directions: *Take the B or Q train to Prospect Park station.*

This tour begins at the busy intersection of Flatbush Avenue, Ocean Avenue, and Empire Boulevard. As you cross Ocean Avenue to the park be mindful of the traffic.

This is the **Willink Entrance (1)**, so named because the Willink estate was here. This entrance was designed by McKim, Mead, and White in 1888. Walk past the two Beaux Arts columns and into the park. Note the yellow brick building on your left (an 1887 Helmle and Huberty work). Restored by the Prospect Park Alliance, this serves as a comfort station and information center.

On the opposite side of the entrance there is a path that will lead you to the **Carousel (2)**. The octagonal red and white brick building was built in 1951. Its 51 animals—horses, deer, lion, giraffe, and dragons—were all hand-carved by Brooklynite Charles Carmel. These were salvaged from two Coney Island merry-go-rounds dated 1915 and 1918. Thanks to the Prospect Park Alliance, in the 1980s the carousel figures were fully restored and painted by Will Morton VIII. For a small fee children of all ages may ride the carousel on weekends and holidays. The facility is also available for private parties (718-965-6512).

Next you'll see a tiny building: the **Flatbush Toll Booth (3)**. Dating from the 1850s, this stood on Flatbush Avenue. The town of Flatbush was independent from the city of Brooklyn and a toll was charged to pass though the town. This is now an information center and gift shop.

Just a few steps away is the **Lefferts Homestead Children's Historic**

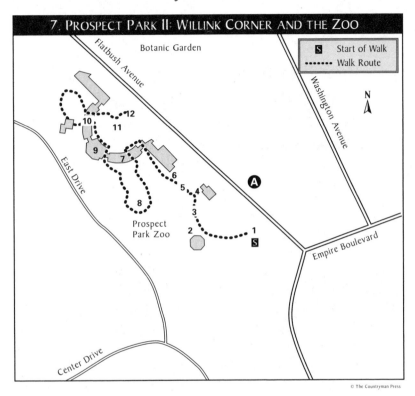

7. PROSPECT PARK II: WILLINK CORNER AND THE ZOO

Botanic Garden

Flatbush Avenue

Washington Avenue

S Start of Walk
•••••• Walk Route

N

A

East Drive

Prospect Park Zoo

Empire Boulevard

Center Drive

© The Countryman Press

House Museum (4). This is the oldest building in Prospect Park. Built by Peter Lefferts in 1777 to replace an earlier house burned during the American Revolution, the house stood on Flatbush Avenue between Maple Street and Midwood Avenue. A shingled house with a gambrel roof supported by six Tuscan colonnettes, it is a typical Dutch colonial farmhouse. The Lefferts family donated the house to the city in 1917 and it was moved to this site. For many years the house museum was staffed by the Daughters of the American Revolution. Now open under the auspices of the Prospect Park Alliance, the museum focuses on Brooklyn rural life in the 1820s and 1830s. It illustrates the lives, not only of Dutch farmers, but also of Native Americans and slaves (www.propsectpark.org; 718-789-2822).

The Lefferts house is just steps away from the **entrance to the Prospect Park Zoo (5)** (www.wcs.org; 718-220-5100). There is a fee to enter the zoo.

As early as 1866, when Prospect Park was in its planning stage, Olmsted and Vaux wanted to include a "Zoological Garden." Though their wishes were never fulfilled, the park early on did include some areas for animals such as a deer paddock, a wild fowl pond, and a flock of sheep to gnaw on the grass blanketing the Long Meadow. By the end of the 19th century, zoos were growing in popularity. In 1890 Prospect Park opened a "Menagerie" located in pens on Sullivan Hill near the Long Meadow. In residence were bears, red and white deer, seals, red foxes, peacocks, a buffalo, and one "sacred cow." The menagerie's population continued to grow through donations of animals when, in 1934, Parks Commissioner Robert Moses proposed to replace it with the Prospect Park Zoo. The land between the former deer paddock to the south and the wild fowl pond to the north was chosen for the zoo. Aymar Embury II was the architect. Six red brick buildings formed a semicircle around the seal pool. The buildings are trimmed with limestone reliefs depicting scenes from Rudyard Kipling's *The Jungle Book*. Work Projects Administration (WPA) artists and laborers were employed on the building project. The Civil Works Administration and the WPA provided funding. When completed in 1935 the facility included a domed elephant house, a lion house, houses for horned animals, birds, and monkeys, and a pit for bears.

In fifty years time the zoo's physical facilities had deteriorated and in 1988 it was closed for a five-year $37 million renovation. In 1993 it reopened under the auspices of the New York Zoological Society. Renamed the "Prospect Park Wildlife Conservation Center," the new name never stuck and it is now again referred to far and wide as the "Prospect Park Zoo." Today the zoo covers 12 acres and is the home to 400 animals representing over 100 species.

After paying the fee, enter the zoo. Note the **steel sculptures (6)** along the way representing fish heads, a chameleon, a snake eating a pig, and a huge octopus.

Two little girls enjoying a ride on the Carousel, stop number 2

Enter the first building on your left: the **World of Animals (7)**. This then leads to the **Discovery Trail (8)** where you will see animals in settings similar to their natural habitats. Among others, the trail will lead you to prairie dogs, porcupines, parma wallabies, and red pandas. Emus, ostriches, bald eagles, and other birds may be seen in the aviary before you complete your walk on the trail.

Enter the next building on your left: **Animal Lifestyles (9).** This large, domed building was originally the elephant house. It is now the home to a troop of hamadryas baboons and their young. The foyer has dioramas entitled Life in the Water, Life in Air, and Life on Land. Other exhibits feature meerkats, emerald tree boas, cotton top tamarins, desert monitors, capybaras, the endangered species the Bali mynah, and other animals.

Continue your odyssey in the next building: **Animals in Our Lives (10)**, which was once the lion house. Among others, there is a Living Color exhibit that features eclectus parrots, green napped rainbow lorikeets, and more creatures. Just north of this building you may visit a working farm with cows, sheep, goats, geese, and ducks. Follow the path around the duck pond.

The **Sea Lions (11)** are, literally, the central attraction at the zoo. Nearby, at the Flatbush Avenue entrance, is the **statue of Lioness and Cubs (12)**. It was modeled by Victor Peter in 1899.

This is the conclusion of this walk. There is a snack stand at the zoo for hungry walkers.

8 · Prospect Park III: Lookout Hill and the Boathouse

Directions: Take the B or Q train to Prospect Park station.

This is a delightful walk that will take you by brooks, wooded knolls, and a scenic outlook and ends at one of Prospect Park's crown jewels: its Boathouse.

Leave the hubbub of the city behind at the **Willink Entrance (1)**, designed by McKim, Mead, and White in 1888. Willink Hill, on your left, was the Willink family estate. But we're walking directly ahead, with the carousel on your right. The path leads to **East Wood Arch (2)**, which dates to 1867 and reflects the Victorian fascination with Middle-Eastern design and motifs.

The arch will lead you to the other side of East Drive. Continue to walk directly ahead. You'll approach the **Lullwater (3)**. Cross it on the **Binnen Bridge (4)** at Binnen Falls. *Binnen* is the Dutch word for "within" and here we are deep within the park.

Take a few steps further and the **Music Pagoda (5)** will be on your right. Built in 1887, its foundation stones were brought from the park's Sullivan Hill (see page 56). This closely resembles a Chinese city gate. The pagoda burned to its stone foundation in 1968. Rebuilt in 1972, it is the venue for concerts and theatrical performances.

On the side of the path opposite the Music Pagoda is the **Nethermead (6)**. Here *nether* means "lower" and *mead* is an abbreviated form of "meadow." Near the center of the park, Nethermead is one of its quietest, most secluded, and least frequented spots. Dog lovers will appreci-

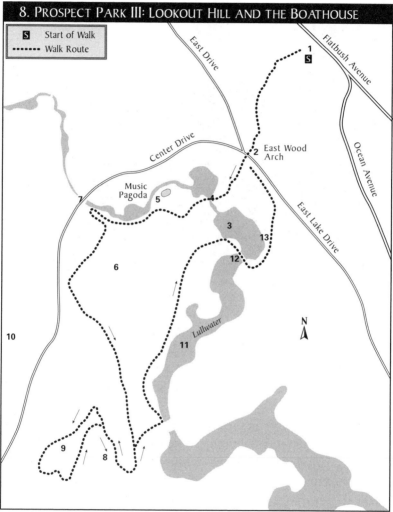

8. PROSPECT PARK III: LOOKOUT HILL AND THE BOATHOUSE

S Start of Walk
•••••• Walk Route

East Drive

Flatbush Avenue

1
S

Center Drive

2 East Wood Arch

Ocean Avenue

East Lake Drive

Music Pagoda

5

4

3

13

7

12

6

Lullwater

10

11

N

9

8

© The Countryman Press

ate that their furry friends are allowed to play off leash in the Nethermead at restricted hours.

Continue on the path and before you are the **Nethermead Arches (7)**, designed by Calvert Vaux in 1879. The Center Drive passes above while

The Boathouse, stop number 13

below the three arches are for the footpath on the left, the bridle path on the right, and the stream between them. The arches have a permanent polychrome of brick, granite, and sandstone.

Do not walk under the Nethermead Arches. Instead, backtrack a few steps and make a right at the Osage orange tree (that is, the second path on your right).

There will be a fork in the path. Bear left at the fork and then walk straight ahead. On your right you will see the **Maryland Monument (8)**. A single classical granite column crowned with a sphere, the memorial was erected in 1895 to honor the Maryland soldiers slaughtered at the Battle of Brooklyn on August 27, 1776. Stanford White designed the monument. It was restored in 1993.

The monument is at the foot of **Lookout Hill (9)**, Prospect Park's highest point. When we were kids growing up in Brooklyn we would call this Lookout "Mountain" and to us city slickers this was the closest thing to a mountain any of us had seen or climbed! Take one of the many paths up the hill. Some were put here as carriage paths; others were conveniently fitted with flights of steps. A century or more ago the top of the hill afforded distant views. Now overgrown with trees, there are partial views from the summit in winter.

Before moving on, look across the drive to **Quaker Hill and the Quaker (Friends) Cemetery (10)**. The cemetery covers 15 acres and its earliest tombstones date to the 1820s. The cemetery is private property and is not open to the public. The actor Montgomery Clift (1920–1966) is buried here, as are members of the Mott family of the apple sauce fortune.

Descend Lookout Hill. Follow the path along Wellhouse Drive as far as Terrace Bridge. Do not cross the bridge. Instead, make a left at the foot of the bridge and follow the path that parallels the **Lullwater (11)**. The path will veer to the right and lead you across the elegant cast iron **Lullwater Bridge (12)** where you will have beautiful views of the Lullwater and of your next destination: the **Boathouse (13)**.

One of the most beloved buildings in Prospect Park, the Boathouse was the work of architects Frank J. Helmle and Ulrich Huberty. Their inspiration was the Library of St. Mark in Venice, designed by Sansovino in the 16th century. The Boathouse was built in 1905. Over the next half century it deteriorated and was slated for demolition in the 1960s. Fortunately it was sparred, rebuilt in 1971, and further restored in 1997–2002. The terra cotta veneer has been completely replaced. Today the Boathouse houses the only urban Audubon Center. A gift shop and snack bar are also here (www.prospectparkaudubon.org; 718-965-8960).

Follow the path back to the East Wood Arch and from there retrace your steps to the Willink entrance.

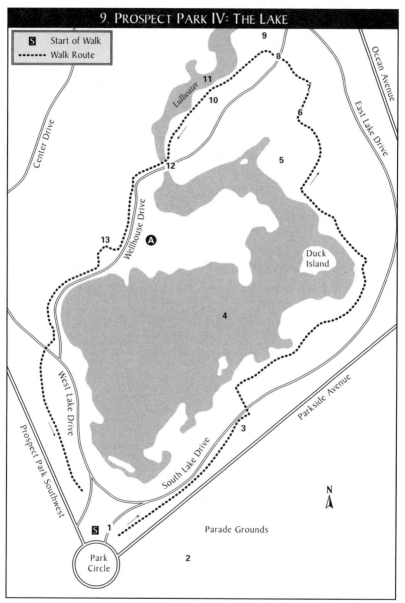

9. PROSPECT PARK IV: THE LAKE

S Start of Walk
••••• Walk Route

9

8

11
Lullwater

10

7

6

12

5

13

A

Duck
Island

4

Ocean Avenue

East Lake Drive

Center Drive

Wellhouse Drive

West Lake Drive

Parkside Avenue

South Lake Drive

Prospect Park Southwest

3

S 1

2

Park
Circle

Parade Grounds

N

© The Countryman Press

9 · Prospect Park IV: The Lake

Directions: Take the F train to Fort Hamilton Parkway.

Walk on Fort Hamilton Parkway to Park Circle. As you cross the street be on the lookout not only for cars but also for horses. The park stables are nearby at Kensington Stables (www.kensingtonstables.com; 718-972-4588) and the horses and their riders enter the park at Park Circle.

The park entrance is flanked by two very dramatic statues entitled the **Horse Tamers (1)**. These were originally called "The Triumph of Mind over Brute Force." The artist was Frederick MacMonnies who also modeled the statues on the arch at Grand Army Plaza. He is best known for his work at the 1897 Chicago Columbian Exposition. Before installation in Prospect Park, the statues were displayed at the Paris Exposition (1900) and the Pan-American Exposition (1901). They stand on pedestals designed by Stanford White.

To the right of the Horse Tamers, across Parkside Avenue, are the **Parade Grounds (2).** Military parades were a popular form of entertainment in the 19th century. As this is no longer so, the rectangular plot is now used for sports and include the Prospect Park Tennis Center, a playground, baseball and softball diamonds, and other playing fields.

Enter the park and take the path that runs parallel with Parkside Avenue. Stop at the **Peristyle (3)**, which is also known as the Croquet Shelter or the Grecian Shelter. Another Stanford White contribution, the terra cotta and limestone shelter dates to 1903.

Cross the South Lake Drive and join the path by the **Lake (4)**. While there are some ponds in Brooklyn (for example at the Green-Wood Cemetery) this is said to be Brooklyn's only lake. Covering 60 acres, it is man-made. You'll probably see a lot of anglers as you walk. I remember when

I was in grade school in the 1950s a highlight of each summer was the fishing contest at the lake sponsored by A&S (Abraham and Strauss Department Store). A&S no longer exists, but Macy's (which bought out A&S) continues the tradition.

As you walk around the lake you will see a number of newly rebuilt rustic shelters for rest, protection from sun and rain, and from which to enjoy idyllic views. Planned by Olmsted and Vaux, these are re-creations of the originals.

The path will lead you to the **Wollman Rink (5)**. Another Robert Moses addition, it was built in 1960. Before that, ice skating on the lake was an annual pastime. The rink is a place for ice skating in winter and pedal boating the rest of the year (718-287-6431).

The rink sits where there once was a "music island." The audience would gather in the **Concert Grove (6)** and face the island, as did the statue of Abraham Lincoln (an 1869 work by H. K. Brown). The other monuments in the concert grove are busts immortalizing great composers such as Mozart, Beethoven, Grieg, and others.

Walk through the concert grove to the **Oriental Pavilion (7)**, or Concert Grove Pavilion. Built in 1874, the pavilion was designed by Vaux himself and borrows from Chinese, Egyptian, and Moorish prototypes. The pavilion burned in 1974 and was meticulously re-created in the 1980s.

At the west end of the Oriental Pavilion there is a broad walkway that leads to the **Cleft Ridge Span (8)**, which was designed by Olmsted and Vaux in 1871. The arch is notable in that it is not stone but rather Beton Coignet. This was an innovative use of molded concrete. Invented in France, this was the first use of Beton Coignet in America.

On leaving the arch note the **Camperdown Elm Tree (9)** on your right with its "weeping" branches. The tree gets its name from Camperdown House in Dundee, Scotland. Curiously, in the early 1800s it was observed that one elm tree on the estate was "weeping." A cutting from the Camperdown Elm was sent to Prospect Park in 1872, which was grafted to the trunk of another elm. The tree has survived through the efforts of folks like poet Marianne Moore and, more recently, the Prospect Park Alliance.

A rustic shelter

The elm is at a fork. Bear left at the fork and walk the path with **Breeze Hill (10)** on your left and the **Lullwater (11)** on your right. Stop at the rustic arbor if you like.

Cross the **Terrace Bridge (12)**.

Detour A: The Peninsula is one of the most remote and least visited areas in the park. Dogs may run free of leashes here during restricted hours. After crossing Terrace Bridge, the path on the left leads you down the Peninsula.

The Terrace Bridge leads to Wellhouse Drive. Walk parallel to the drive. You will see the **Wellhouse (13)** on your right at the foot of Lookout Hill. The Wellhouse was built in 1869. A Calvert and Vaux design, its stone and brick walls are 2 feet thick. It housed a pumping system that supplied well water to Prospect Park. The park now gets its water from the city and the well is no longer in use.

Walk to the end of Wellhouse Drive. Cross West Drive at the cross-walk and exit to Prospect Park Southwest.

COURTESY OF PROSPECT PARK ALLIANCE

10 · Eastern Parkway

Directions: Take the 2 or 3 line to Eastern Parkway/Brooklyn Museum subway station.

Eastern Parkway is a 2-mile stretch that runs from Grand Army Plaza to Ralph Avenue. America's first parkway, it was planned and developed in the 1860s by Frederick Law Olmsted and Calvert Vaux. Both men created Prospect Park, and their larger plan was to have several similar parkways radiating from Grand Army Plaza. The only other parkway in Brooklyn that was realized is Ocean Parkway, which, by the way, has the nation's oldest bicycle path.

All of the stops on this walk are in "Institute Park"—a term that is rarely heard nowadays. The neighborhood across the parkway (Prospect Heights) was very fashionable a century ago. In the 1920s mansions were replaced by luxury apartment buildings. Though the neighborhood declined in the second half of the 20th century, it is now improving: old apartment buildings are being renovated and newer ones are being built.

One such apartment building was lived in by one-time World Chess Champion Bobby Fischer (1943–2008). He lived at 560 Lincoln Place, Apartment Q. The great American composer Aaron Copland (1900–1990) grew up in Prospect Heights. The 1990s TV series *Brooklyn South* was shot in this neighborhood. And the movie *The Tenant* (1970) was filmed here, too.

This walking tour begins before you leave the **subway station (1)**. The IRT line was extended along Eastern Parkway in 1920. Some 83 years later—in 2003—this station was rehabilitated and a permanent installation of artwork was added. On exiting the station you'll see a display of architectural elements that are part of the Brooklyn Museum's collec-

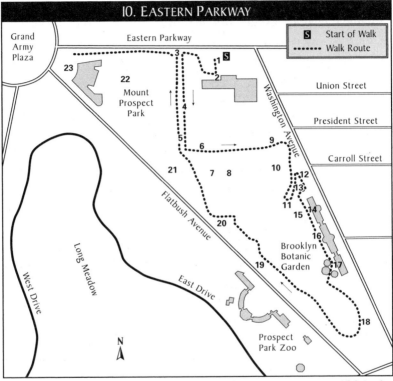

10. EASTERN PARKWAY

Grand Army Plaza

Eastern Parkway

S Start of Walk
•••••• Walk Route

23

22
Mount Prospect Park

Union Street

President Street

Carroll Street

Washington Avenue

21

Flatbush Avenue

West Drive

Long Meadow

East Drive

Brooklyn Botanic Garden

Prospect Park Zoo

N

© The Countryman Press

tion. These molded terra cotta borders, plaques, lunettes, keystones, and other forms have been salvaged from demolished New York buildings and now adorn the walls of what might have been an otherwise plain and uninspiring subway stop.

Emerge from the subway. Looming before you is the massive façade of the **Brooklyn Museum (2)** (www.brooklynmuseum.org; 718-638-5000).

The roots of the Brooklyn Museum can be traced to humble beginnings in 1825. The Marquis de Lafayette laid the cornerstone of what was then the Brooklyn Apprentices' Library. Among the witnesses gathered for the occasion was a six-year-old Brooklyn boy named Walt Whitman. In 1831 the Apprentices' Library and the Brooklyn Lyceum joined to form the Brooklyn Institute. This blossomed into the Brooklyn Institute of Arts and Sciences in 1893, which was the umbrella organization for the Brooklyn Museum, the Brooklyn Academy of Music, the Brooklyn Botanic Garden, and the Brooklyn Children's Museum. All four cultural institutions exist today, though now each is independent.

When designed by McKim, Mead, and White in 1895 the plan was to create the largest museum in the world, consisting of four wings surrounding a central courtyard and housing not only art but also science and natural history collections. As it is, one side of the proposed Beaux Arts building museum was completed between 1897 and 1925. At first the main entrance was through the colonnaded portico on the third floor, which was reached by way of a long magisterial flight of steps. In the 1930s a WPA project was to modernize the museum in part by removing the grand staircase, adding a new entrance at ground level, and updating the gallery spaces and lighting.

Before entering the museum note the figures on the façade in the pediment and the tops of the columns. These were the work of Daniel Chester French who also modeled the seated president at Washington's Lincoln Memorial. To the left and to the right of the entrance pavilion there are allegorical figures representing Brooklyn and Manhattan, also by French. They once flanked the entrance to the Manhattan Bridge and were moved here in 1964.

In 1986, as the 21st century approached, the museum's board of trustees sought a master plan for renovation and growth. The winning plan was submitted by the partnership of Arata Isozaki and James Stewart Polshek. The auditorium was added and the west wing renovated. Finally, in 2001, the new glass and steel entrance pavilion, surrounded by a plaza and fountains, was opened.

The Brooklyn Museum's art collection is one of the largest and most diverse in the world. It is the second largest museum in New York City and the seventh in size in America. The permanent collection consists of more than one and a half million objects. These include one of the finest

Egyptology collections in the world, and collections of pre-Columbian, American, African, Native American, Asian, classical, Middle Eastern, Islamic, European, contemporary, and feminist art. All this is housed in a 560,000-square-foot building. The annual visitation is about one million. And the Brooklyn Museum has the fifth largest art museum library in America.

More specific to Brooklyn, two early Brooklyn houses have been reconstructed in the museum and are on permanent display. These are the Jan Martense Schenck House, which dates to about 1675, and the Nicholas Schenck House, which was built about 1775.

You saw some salvaged architectural details in the subway station. If you would like to see more of the same, walk to the back of the museum and visit the sculpture garden. It has an extensive collection of terra cotta, limestone, cast iron, and marble artwork saved from buildings that were built from 1880 to 1910. These include pieces from the old Pennsylvania Station and Coney Island's Steeplechase Park. Some of the art was sculpted by well-known artists Daniel Chester French, Gutzon Borglum (who modeled Mount Rushmore), and Karl Bitter.

The Brooklyn Museum has a café and the Museum Shop.

After the museum continue your walk along Eastern Parkway. Facing the parkway, turn left. After just a few steps you will be at the **Brooklyn Botanic Garden (3)** (www.bbg.org; 718-623-7200). The entrance was designed by Polshek Partnership Architects LLP in 2005.

The Brooklyn Botanic Garden was opened in 1910. Philanthropist Alfred T. White provided $25,000 in seed money, which was matched by the city of New York. When opened the garden included 39 acres and was expanded to the present 52 acres by 1914. At first the Olmsted brothers—Frederick Jr. and John Charles, sons of Frederick Law Olmsted who designed Prospect Park—made plans for the garden. But it was Harold Caparn who became the mastermind behind the garden, working as its chief landscape architect from 1912 to 1945. Caparn's vision was a garden that would be both beautiful and useful as a teaching tool.

The garden has grown (literally) to include more than 12,000 plant

ROBERT I. REGALBUTO

Brooklyn Museum

species. It would be impossible to see the entire garden in one visit. So, too, each season buds with a wide variety of blossoms to please the eye: lilacs, daffodils, tulips, and cherry blossoms in the spring, roses and perennials in summer, vibrant foliage and mums in the fall, and the greenhouse vegetation in winter. With this in mind, the walking tour in this book presents an introductory overview of the Brooklyn Botanic Garden.

Enter the garden from Eastern Parkway, paying the fee. The extensive lawn in front of you is the **Osborne Garden (4)**. Walk the length of the lawn on the grass or on one of the paths, enjoying the sight and scent of crab apples, wisterias, and azaleas along the way. The limestone fountain at the end of the lawn is typical of formal Italian gardens like this one, combining stone, water, and plantings. Take a seat on one of the **limestone benches (5)**. But be careful of what you say. These are "whispering chairs" and just a whisper can be heard at the seat across the way. Whispering chairs were a favorite garden feature in Elizabethan England.

Walk down the broad flight of steps. Make an immediate left to the path that will lead you to the **Overlook (6)**. The lilac collection will be on your right. Beyond the lilacs, also on your right, will be the **Cranford Rose Garden (7)**. The rose garden was a gift of Walter Cranford, an engineer who made his fortune expanding the New York subway system. Opened in 1928, the rose garden has almost 1,200 varieties of roses and more than 5,000 rose bushes. Most of the roses have been cultivated to bloom in June and again in September. The rose garden pavilion was restored in 2006.

Next you'll see the **Cherry Esplanade (8)**, which blooms in April. This is the site of the annual Sakura Matsuri Festival, which is a celebration of not only the cherry blossoms but also Japanese art, music, and dance.

The path will lead you to the **Herb Garden (9)**, also on your right. This was a WPA project in the 1930s. It has over 300 herb plants.

The path you have been following will now join another that will curve to the right. This brings you to another highlight: the **Japanese Hill-and-Pond Garden (10)**. Since its opening in 1915, the Japanese garden has been a perennial favorite with visitors. The landscape artist was Takeo Shiota. Tragically, in 1943 he died in a South Carolina internment camp for Japanese Americans.

Note the stone lantern at the garden's entrance. Known as a "shogun" lantern, this dates to the year 1652. In 1980 it was a gift from New York's sister city, Tokyo.

Enter the Japanese garden and view the pond from the wooden pavilion. Note the torii gate in the pond, and the granite Shinto shrine and footbridge on the opposite shore.

The Japanese Hill-and-Pond Garden was restored in 2000 at a cost of $3.2 million.

On leaving the Japanese garden turn right. The second path on your right is the **Celebrity Path (11)**. Begun in 1985 through the generosity of the Brooklyn Union Gas Company, it is a series of more than 100 concrete pavers, each honoring a notable person who was born in Brooklyn or who has lived here. New pavers (and honorees) are added every year.

Backtrack to the beginning of the Celebrity Path. Take a few more steps and on your right take the path that leads to the **Shakespeare Garden (12)**. Opened in 1920, it was the gift of Henry C. Folger who founded Washington's Folger Shakespeare Library. Based on English cottage gardens, many of its plants are mentioned in the Bard's plays.

The path in the Shakespeare Garden leads to the **Fragrance Garden (13)**. This garden is unusual in that the beds are atop 28-inch-high walls. Installed in 1955, it was one of the country's first gardens designed specifically for the blind. They—and all visitors—are encouraged to touch and feel the plants and to smell their scents.

You entered the Fragrance Garden from the north (or 12 o'clock) position. Exit the garden at 9 o'clock (i.e., the west side) and then turn left. The building on your left is the **Visitor Center (14)**. Another McKim, Mead, and White work, it was built in 1918. Over the years this has served as an administration building, a laboratory, and a school. Enter for more information on the garden and its programs.

The visitor center faces **Magnolia Plaza (15)**, which is alive with blossoms from March through June. In the center of the plaza is an armillary sphere and compass.

Facing the sphere turn left and walk to the **Lily Pool Terrace (16).** It parallels the Palm House, which was built in 1914 as the garden's first conservatory. The Palm House is now available to the public for parties and special events. A perennial garden borders the front of it.

Beyond the Palm House is the gift shop, where books, publications, plants, and other garden-related goods are sold.

You have arrived at the **Steinhardt Conservatory complex (17)**, which was built in 1988. On entering the conservatory follow the Trail of Evolution exhibit. To the left of the trail you will see the Bonsai Museum. While the garden has a collection of 600 of these miniatured trees, about 100 are on display at any given time. Next is the Robert W. Wilson Aquatic House, followed by the Desert Pavilion and then the Tropical

ROBERT J. REGALBUTO

Lily Pool Terrace, stop number 16, Brooklyn Botanic Garden

Pavilion. Finally, there is the Helen V. Mattin Warm Temperate Pavilion.

The Terrace Café is adjacent to the Desert Pavilion.

Take the flight of steps between the Desert Pavilion and the Tropical Pavilion. There will be a cross path. Turn left at the cross. This will lead you to the **Children's Garden (18)**. Dating to 1914, this was the first garden in America cultivated specifically to educate children. Each year 500 children ages 3 to 17 plant, tend, and harvest flowers and vegetables. The adjacent Discovery Garden is a fun place for toddlers to explore and learn.

The path in front of the Children's Garden curves to the right and leads you past a stream, fields, olive trees, a peony and iris garden, and honeysuckle trees. On your left will be the **Rock Garden (19)**. Its 18 boulders (or glacial erratics) were found on this site. A plaque on each identifies the type of rock and the distance from the point of origin before its journey here by glacier.

Continue your walk north and note the willow trees on your right. The path culminates at the **Rose Arc Pool (20)** at the Cherry Esplanade. At the straight side of the pool turn left and follow the path past the Cranford Rose Garden and then onto the **Native Flora Garden (21)**, which will be on your left. Walk through the beautifully crafted rustic wooden gates. The garden dates to 1911. Its plantings have been gathered from within a radius of 100 miles of Brooklyn. Various "habitats" are presented: pine barrens, limestone ledge, bog, dry meadow, kettle pond, serpentine rock formation, wet meadow, and deciduous woodland.

From the Native Flora Garden turn left and the path will lead you back to Eastern Parkway.

On leaving the Brooklyn Botanic Garden turn left and on your left will be **Mount Prospect Park (22)**, which is the second highest point in Brooklyn. (The highest point is Battle Hill in the Green-Wood Cemetery.) Now heavily wooded, in colonial times the mount was relatively clear of vegetation and offered 360-degree views of the region as far as New Jersey in the west and Long Island to the east; hence the name "prospect." During the American Revolution the Continental Army used this as an outlook. In 1856 a reservoir was built on the mount, with a water tower next to it. The tower was demolished in 1940 and the reservoir filled in to accommodate a playground on its site. Under Mayor Giuliani the park was restored in 2001.

Continue your walk westerly along Eastern Parkway to its end at Grand Army Plaza. On your left is the Main Branch of the **Brooklyn Public**

Library (23) (www.brooklynpubliclibrary.org; 718-230-2100). The library had a small start in 1897 when it began in modest, though picturesque, surroundings in a Bedford Avenue wood schoolhouse surrounded by a cornfield. Between 1901 and 1923 Andrew Carnegie donated $1.6 million to the fledgling library system and built 21 branches. Carnegie's generosity in building libraries in Brooklyn and elsewhere (over 2,500 libraries worldwide) justifiably earned him the title Patron Saint of Libraries. Today the "BPL" has 60 branches throughout the borough, each within a half mile of every residence. It is the fifth largest public library system in America with a collection of 3 million books and other materials. The library also houses the Brooklyn Collection, the Brooklyn Photography Collection (with over 25,000 photographs), and the archives of the *Brooklyn Daily Eagle*—a newspaper that stopped publication in 1955.

The first library building on this site was begun in 1912. It was to be a Beaux Arts building similar in style to the Brooklyn Museum. Only one wing, parallel to Eastern Parkway, was built. The original plan was abandoned and replaced in 1941 with the present Art Moderne library that was influenced by the Paris Exposition in 1937. The architects were Alfred Morton Githens and Francis Keally. The library building was designed to resemble an open book: the "spine" of the book is the concave façade facing Grand Army Plaza, and the book's "covers" run along Eastern Parkway and Flatbush Avenue. Before entering the library note the gilded reliefs carved on either side of the doors, representing the arts and the sciences. They are the work of C. Paul Jennewein who created similar art for Manhattan's Rockefeller Center.

Between the reliefs there is a bronze screen divided into fifteen panels. If you look closely you may be able to identify literary characters on the screen, such as Rip Van Winkle. You'll also see a raven (from Edgar Allen Poe's poem) and a whale (Herman Melville's *Moby Dick*). The screen was modeled by Thomas Hudson Jones whose work also may be seen at the Tomb of the Unknown Soldier at Arlington National Cemetery.

Enter the library. You'll pass though an "outer temple" and into the great hall—all of which is paneled with Appalachian white oak. The building was enlarged in 1956, 1972, and 1989. About a million and a half cardholders visit this library every year.

This is where the Eastern Parkway tour ends. Information on Grand Army Plaza is at the beginning of the Prospect Park I chapter in this guide.

II · Prospect Park West

Directions: *Take the 2 or 3 train to Grand Army Plaza.*

T his walk is my personal favorite in this book. Growing up just a few steps from Prospect Park West, I considered the park my playground. As a small boy I walked on top of the stone wall on Prospect Park West more times than I can remember. And then there were the walks to the end of the street with my mother where we would continue on to the Brooklyn Museum.

To start the walk, leave the Grand Army Plaza subway station and walk south along Plaza Street West. After you cross Union Street you will be at the beginning of Prospect Park West. At first (before there was a Prospect Park) this was known as Ninth Avenue. The large building at **35 Prospect Park West (1)** between Union and President Streets was built in the 1920s as office space for the Knights of Columbus, a Roman Catholic fraternal organization. In 1962 the Knights sold the property to the Carmelite Sisters for the Aged and Infirm. It then became the Madonna Residence—a retirement home. The sisters sold the facility to DLK Ventures in 1996 for $3.3 million. Renovated, this is now the Prospect Park Residence—a nondenominational retirement home.

Walk south. Stop at **numbers 18 and 19 (2)** Prospect Park West and note the Renaissance Revival townhouses built in 1898 to plans by Montrose W. Morris. The limestone façade at #19 features a rusticated ground floor and a Palladian window: a design of the 16th-century Italian architect Andrea Palladio.

Continue south along this, the outskirts of the "Gold Coast of Brooklyn." The **Henry Hulbert House (3)** is at the corner of First Street (49 Prospect Park West). This is not one but two houses, built in 1892 for

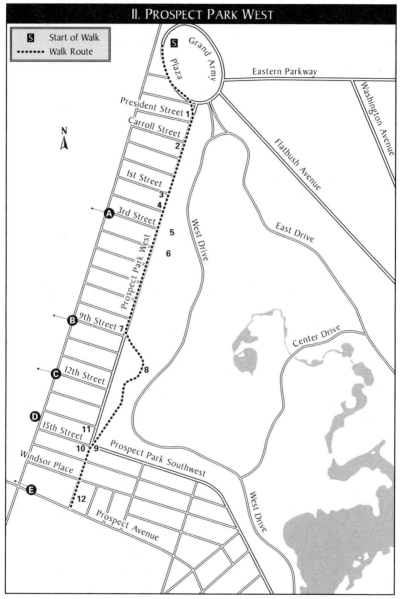

II. PROSPECT PARK WEST

S Start of Walk
······ Walk Route

Grand Army Plaza

Eastern Parkway

Washington Avenue

President Street **1**

Carroll Street **2**

1st Street **3**
4

A 3rd Street

Prospect Park West

West Drive

5

6

Flatbush Avenue

East Drive

Center Drive

B 9th Street **7**

C 12th Street **8**

D 15th Street **11**

10 **9** Prospect Park Southwest

Windsor Place

E **12**

Prospect Avenue

West Drive

N

© The Countryman Press

Hulbert (north side) and his daughter and her husband (south side). The twin houses were designed in Romanesque Revival style by Montrose W. Morris. Hulbert made his money in paper supplies. For fifty years (1927–1977) the houses were the Ethical Culture School. They then became the Woodward School. It is now the Poly Prep Lower School (see page 114).

The next mansion at #53 is the **Brooklyn Ethical Culture Society Meeting House (4)**, one-time home to William H. Childs, the founder of the Bon Ami Cleaning Powder Company. The architect was William B. Tubby. Here he borrowed from 17th-century English prototypes and created a Jacobean-style manor. It was built in 1901. Note the lovely gardens that surround the house.

Walk just one more block and you'll be at the **Third Street entrance (5)** to Prospect Park. The statues of two proud panthers flank the entrance as if to guard it.

Detour A: To view a bit of American Revolutionary War history, walk down Third Street four long blocks to the Old Stone House at the corner of Fifth Avenue. Built in 1699 for Dutch settler Claes Arentson Vechte, the house was occupied by the British during the Battle of Brooklyn (1776). Sold to another Dutch family, the Cortelyous, in 1797, the Old Stone House is also known as the Vechte-Cortelyou House. Real estate developer Edwin C. Litchfield owned the property for a time in the mid-19th century. It later was the clubhouse for the team that became the Brooklyn Dodgers; they played in nearby Washington Park. Sadly, the house was demolished in 1897. It was rebuilt in the 1930s about twenty feet from the first site. The original stones (which were buried here) were used in the reconstruction. Neglected for many years, the house was restored in 1997. It is now the Old Stone House Historic Interpretive Center (www.theoldstonehouse.org; 718-768-3195).

To continue the main walking tour, do not enter the park, but walk south for just another block or so. The **Litchfield Villa (6)** will be on your left. Edwin Clark Litchfield was an attorney who made his fortune, in part, by investing in Midwestern railroads. He was also a real estate

Marquis de Lafayette Monument, stop number 7

developer and owned much of what we now know as Park Slope. His landholdings stretched from First to Ninth Streets and from Tenth Avenue (which existed "on paper"—it was never paved and is a part of the park) to the Gowanus Creek (which he transformed into an industrial canal). He had this mansion built between 1854–1857. The estate was named "Grace Hill" in honor of his wife, Grace Hill Hubbard Litchfield. The architect chosen was Alexander Jackson Davis who was responsible for many mansions in the Hudson River Valley. This house is Italianate and as such includes many features of Tuscan farmhouses: a large central tower, round-top windows, a low-pitched roof, and widely hanging eaves with decorative brackets. Once the center of Brooklyn's antebellum social life, the estate had unobstructed views of Upper New York Bay. In 1869 the property was bought to be included in the then-developing Prospect Park. The Litchfields, however, continued to live here as tenants, until Grace's death in 1881. This is now used as office space and is the park's administration building.

Walk just four more blocks to Ninth Street, which divides the North and South Slopes. There you will see the **Marquis de Lafayette Monument (7)**. Dedicated in 1917, this has a connection to the Lincoln Memorial in Washington, DC. Both were designed by architect Henry Bacon and both this sculpture and the seated Abraham Lincoln are the work of Daniel Chester French (though here French was assisted by Augustus Lukeman).

Detour B: Before entering the park you may want to consider taking a walk down Ninth Street to a pristine example of a Brooklyn Victorian house. The William B. Cronyn House (1855) is at 271 Ninth Street (between Fifth and Fourth Avenues). The house is freestanding and is crowned with a well-preserved cast iron crest on a slate roof. Surprisingly, the house was designed by Patrick C. Keely whose forte was Gothic Revival churches. Cronyn's house later became the Charles M. Higgins Ink Factory. The walk on Ninth Street is a pleasant one with many architectural surprises along the way. For example, there is a Beaux Arts gem of a library at Ninth Street and Sixth Avenue. It was built in 1906 through the generosity of Andrew Carnegie.

Detour C: The former Ansonia Clock Company Factory is on Seventh Avenue between 12th and 13th Streets. The factory dates to 1881 and at one time employed about 1,500 workers, most of whom were Polish and Irish immigrants. After closing in 1930 the factory stood empty for 50 years. In 1982 it was converted into condominiums. It is now known as Ansonia Court.

Returning to the main tour: Walk around the Lafayette Monument and enter Prospect Park. The path on your right will lead you to the **Bandshell (8)**. It was built in 1939 replacing a hockey rink and a place for archery. This was another Robert Moses project. The architect was Aymar Embury II who also designed the zoos in this park and in Central Park. In recent years the bandshell and the surrounding playgrounds have been remodeled and expanded.

Take one of the paths south and exit the park at the **twin pillars (9)**. These are copies of the Acanthus Column of Delphi (Greece) built in the 4th century B.C. The acanthus leaf was a very popular classical decorative motif. These granite columns were designed by Stanford White in 1906. Each is topped with a replica of an ancient lantern.

Leave the park and face **Bartel-Pritchard Circle (10)**, which is named for two neighborhood men killed in World War I. Prospect Park West continues beyond the circle and in fact becomes the "Main Street" for this neighborhood. The author Pete Hamill grew up here and this is the setting for his novel *The Gift*.

The **Pavilion Theatre (11)** stands at the circle. In 1908 brothers Rudolph and Harry Sanders opened a nickelodeon on this spot. This developed into the 500-seat Marathon Theatre. Then in 1928 the brothers demolished the Marathon and built the 1,500-seat Sanders Theatre. The architect was Edward Kleinert and he embellished the interior with a Moorish/Middle Eastern décor. Patrons were entertained with the sound of a Wurlitzer two-manual, seven-rank organ (Opus 1816). The organ was removed by the time I went to matinees here as a kid. I remember the tickets were 50 cents and all the movies would have been rated "G" (had there been a rating system at that time). The Sanders Theatre closed in 1978 and stood empty for nearly 20 years. Only a skeleton remained of its marquee. The theater was renovated and reopened in 1996 as the Pavilion Theatre. It has nine screens today (718-369-0838).

Detour D: It is a very short walk from the circle down 15th Street to the corner of Eighth Avenue. There you'll see the 14th Regiment Armory, New York National Guard. The fortresslike armory dates to 1895; William A. Mundell was the architect. The 14th Regiment was formed in 1847 and fought in the Civil War, the Spanish American War, and World War I. A statue of a doughboy guards the entrance door. It was sculpted in 1923 by Anton Scaaf. No longer used by the National Guard, the future of the armory is uncertain.

Back to the subject of movies. The film *As Good As It Gets* was filmed in part in this neighborhood. The 1997 movie starred Jack Nicholson and Helen Hunt who won the Academy Award for best actor and best actress. They also garnered Golden Globe Awards as did the film for best motion picture (musical or comedy). Among other spots in the neighborhood, some scenes were shot at Farrell's Bar at the corner of 16th Street (718-788-8779). Shirley MacLaine had a drink at Farrell's while filming *Desperate Characters* here in 1971. Other movies shot in the neighborhood were *Dog Day Afternoon* (1975) with Al Pacino, *Blue in the Face* (1995), and *Smoke* (1995).

Walk along Prospect Park West. The Windsor Terrace neighborhood is on your left. Beyond Windsor Place on your left you will see a full block of buildings belonging to **Holy Name Church (12)** (Roman Catholic). This includes the elementary school built in 1923 from which I graduated in 1964. The Gothic Revival church dates to 1878. Sadly, about a century later, despite the protest of parishioners, the hierarchy stripped the interior of its 19th-century treasures and artifacts without regard for artistic or sentimental value.

This is where this tour ends. There are entrances to the 15th Street–Prospect Park subway station (F line) on Windsor Place and at the circle.

Detour E: It is a walk of four long blocks downhill on Prospect Avenue to Grand Prospect Hall (www.grandprospect.com; 718-788-0777). The hall is at 263 Prospect Avenue near Fifth Avenue. The first Prospect Hall was built on this site in 1892. After it burned the present one was built in 1903. The architect was Ulrich J. Huberty. It was, and is, a lavish place for entertaining and includes a roof garden, a Bavarian beer hall, and a vast ballroom measuring 125 feet long, 75 feet wide, and 40 feet from floor to ceiling. The elegant interior has been the backdrop to several films including *The Cotton Club* (1984), *Prizzi's Honor* (1985), and *The Royal Tenenbaums* (2001). The closest subway stop is one block away at Prospect Avenue and Fourth Avenue (R and M lines).

12 · Flatbush

Directions: Take the Q or B train to Church Avenue.

Flatbush was settled by the Dutch in 1634. It was one of six towns that eventually became the borough of Brooklyn. When chartered, it was named "Vlacke Bos," which is translated "wooded plain." The English took possession of the Dutch colony in 1664 and anglicized the name to Flat Bush.

Flatbush remained rural through the 19th century. Fiercely independent, Flatbush imposed a toll on those entering the town. One of the toll booths today is preserved in Prospect Park (see page 57). In 1874 its citizens refused to be joined to the city of Brooklyn. Finally in 1894 Flatbush joined Brooklyn and in 1898 became a part of Greater New York.

It was the advent of the electrified Brighton Line that led to the growth of Flatbush in the early 20th century. This became a largely Jewish community. That has changed as African Americans and diverse immigrant groups now populate Flatbush.

After World War I the song *Nesting Time in Flatbush* became popular. Flatbush became the setting for several movies. In the 1940s *It Happened in Flatbush* and *Whistling in Brooklyn* (starring Red Skelton and the Brooklyn Dodgers) took place here. As times changed, *The Lords of Flatbush* (1974) presented an updated Flatbush, starring Sylvester Stallone and Henry Winkler.

Perhaps Flatbush's best-known citizen is Mary Tyler Moore—"America's Sweetheart"—and Brooklyn's!

As in many inner city areas, it is wise to take precautions while visiting today's Flatbush. Be sure to visit during daylight hours and, if possible, include a walking companion.

On leaving the **subway station (1)** turn left and walk along Church Avenue. Originally known as Church Lane, this street dates from the 1600s and was lined with many old homes. These were replaced with stores after the Brighton Line "suburban railroad" arrived in the early 20th century.

Ahead, on your right, is Church Avenue's namesake: the former **Flatbush Reformed Dutch Church (2)**, which was founded by Governor Peter Stuyvesant in 1654. This site is the oldest in continuous use for a church in New York City. The first churches were built in 1654 and 1702. This building was completed in 1798. The architect was Thomas Fardon, the style is Georgian, and the building material is fieldstone. Note the wooden octagonal steeple that is surrounded by colonnettes and urns. The tower houses a bell that dates to 1796. Cast in Holland, the bell was seized in transit by British forces who brought it to Nova Scotia. Once finally in place in the belfry here, the bell was tolled when George Washington died in 1799 and has been tolled on the death of every president since.

The Dutch and their descendants have long since left Flatbush, and the church now belongs to the Bethel Presbyterian Reformed Church, Inc.

You are at the intersection of Church Avenue and Flatbush Avenue. Before the arrival of the Europeans Flatbush Avenue was an Indian path. This was later named Main Street, then Flatbush Road, and today is Flatbush Avenue.

Standing on the steps of the church look across Flatbush Avenue to your right to your next stop: **Erasmus Hall (3)**, which stands on land donated by the Reformed Dutch Church. Cross Flatbush Avenue and stand at the entrance arch to Erasmus Hall.

Erasmus Hall Academy was founded as a private secondary school for boys in 1787. The oldest high school in New York State and the second oldest in America, this is known as the "mother of high schools." New York Governor George Clinton and John Jay (first chief justice of the United States) were among the school's founders, as were Vice President Aaron Burr and Alexander Hamilton (first U.S. secretary of the treasury). Later, in less friendly times, Burr killed Hamilton in a duel in Weehawken, New Jersey (1804).

Look through the arch. The bronze statue is a depiction of Desiderius Erasmus (1466–1536). He was a Dutch humanist and theologian who helped bring the Renaissance to England during the time of King Henry VIII. The statue is a copy of a 1622 original (Hendrick de Keiser, sculptor) that stands in Rotterdam, Erasmus's home town.

The white Federal building in back of the statue is the original academy building. It dates to 1787. Note the hand-carved clapboards. The attic was known as "the brig" where boys were held in solitary confinement for breaking the school rules. Others were whipped. The academy's Rule

Number Nine stipulated that: "No student shall be permitted to practise any species of gaming nor to drink any spirituous liquors nor to go into any tavern in Flat Bush without obtaining consent of a teacher."

Erasmus Hall's first class had an enrollment of 26 boys, each paying six pounds sterling in tuition. Students eventually came from distant places: New Orleans, the West Indies, Cuba, Mexico, Brazil, Sweden, France, Spain, and Portugal. Girls began to enroll in the early 19th century. In 1895 the school was given to the City of Brooklyn and Erasmus Hall Academy became Erasmus Hall High School. Ten years later a Collegiate Gothic building surrounded the 1787 academy and its green. The architect was C. B. J. Snyder who designed many New York City high school buildings.

Over the past two centuries about a quarter million students have graduated from Erasmus Hall. Some of the better known are Mae West, Barbra Streisand, Barbara Stanwyck (aka Ruby Stevens), Eli Wallach, Susan Hayward (aka Edythe Marrenner), Lainie (Levine) Kazan, actor Bernard Koppel ("Doc" on *The Love Boat* TV series), cartoonist Joseph R. Barbera, travel publisher Arthur Frommer, comedian Marty Engels, journalist and TV personality Dorothy Kilgallen, Al Davis (owner of the Oakland Raiders), Janelle Commissiong (1977 Miss Universe), Olympic medalist Cheryl Toussaint, real estate developer Samuel LeFrak, author Mickey Spillane, author and rabbi Harold Kushner, Arthur Sackler (art collector and major benefactor to the Metropolitan Museum and the Smithsonian), and Nobel prize winner Dr. Eric Kandel. Opera singer Beverly Sills attended Erasmus Hall and then graduated from another school, as did singer/songwriter Neil Diamond. World chess champion Bobby Fischer chose to leave Erasmus Hall before graduation to devote more time to perfect his game. Moses Harry Horwitz dropped out in 1915 after attending Erasmus Hall for two months. He later used the stage name Moe Howard and became one of the Three Stooges.

Erasmus Hall High School per se ceased to exist in 1994 when the campus was divided into several specialized secondary schools.

After seeing Erasmus Hall, stand at the arch facing Flatbush Avenue.

Erasmus Hall arch entrance, stop number 3

Turn left and walk to the next corner (Snyder Avenue). "Snyder" is the Dutch word for tailor, and the street was named after an early Flatbush family. Turn left on Snyder Avenue and, on your left, at #35 is **Flatbush Town Hall (4)** (built 1874–1875). It is a stately reminder that, until 1894, Flatbush was a town independent of the city of Brooklyn. This is a work of John Y. Culyer, who was an associate of Frederick Law Olmsted and Calvert Vaux—the creators of Prospect Park. This red brick building is a High Victorian Gothic design. Note the stone pointed arches, the "drip moldings" atop the doors and windows, and the decorative "bosses" (carved blocks). Town Hall served Flatbush well as a courthouse, police station, and as a community center. The ballroom on the second floor hosted many parties—including one to celebrate Erasmus Hall's centennial in 1887.

Facing Snyder Avenue turn right and return to Flatbush Avenue. Cross Flatbush Avenue and turn left. The next street on your right will be Albemarle Road, named for the Kensington, London, street honoring the Duke of Albemarle. Walk down Albemarle Road just a few short steps and make a right on East 21st Street. You are entering the Albemarle-Kensington Terraces Historic District. After a few paces on East 21st Street make a right onto **Albemarle Terrace (5)**. This cul-de-sac has a series of charming Georgian-style townhouses designed in 1916 by Brooklyn architects Slee and Bryson.

Continue on East 21st Street to the next cul-de-sac: **Kenmore Terrace (6).** On your left, at 2101-2103, was the parsonage for the Reformed Dutch church. Built in 1853, it is a Greek Revival house. Note the Corinthian columns on the veranda and the dentil molding above. The parsonage originally stood at 900 Flatbush Avenue and was moved to this site in 1918.

Continue in the same direction on East 21st Street, walking past the churchyard with its ancient gravestones, some of which date to the 1600s. Make a left and walk four blocks along an unappealing stretch of Church Avenue until you reach Buckingham Road. There you will be delightfully surprised—and rewarded—by the sight of the houses before you. This enclave is known as Kensington, named after a fashionable London borough. In 1898 the developer Dean Alvord bought 40 acres from the Reformed Dutch Church and also bought Bergen farm. He built the area you are about to explore, giving the streets distinctively English names. Alvord hired architect John J. Petit. He and his associates designed most of these houses, in a variety of architectural styles. Kensington has been designated the Prospect Park South Historic District.

Two movies were filmed, in part, in Kensington: *Sophie's Choice* (1982) starring Meryl Streep and Kevin Kline, and *Reversal of Fortune* (1990). *Sophie's Choice* was based on William Styron's novel of the same name, which is set in Flatbush.

Walk down Buckingham Road. The **William H. McEntee House (7)** is at #115. It is a 1900 Shingle Style house. The Shingle Style became very popular in the late 1800s and drew on many earlier influences: for example, the shingles recall the houses of colonial America, the Palladian (triple) windows on the third floor are based on designs of the 16th-century Italian architect Andrea Palladio, and the corner bell-shaped tower is borrowed from medieval French sources.

Next is the George U. Tompers House at #125 and, after that, the **Japanese House (8)** at #131. This was built for Frederick Strange Kolle in 1902. Kolle was a German doctor who invented the X-ray. Petit worked with three Japanese artisans in creating this house. Its roof was originally covered with Japanese tiles.

The **William A. Norwood House (9)** stands at #143. It is a 1906 Italianate design by Walter A. Cassin. Across the street, at #104, there stands the **Russell Benedict House (10)**, a 1902 Petit work.

When you reach the corner you will be at Albemarle Road. The **L. McDonald House (11)** is at 1518 Albemarle—a 1902 "Chicago School" design.

Turn right onto Albemarle Road and walk toward Marlborough Road. On your left, at 1510, you'll see the **Maurice Minton House (12),** which is a copy of the Temple of Vesta in Rome. The 1902 house was built complete with horse stable and a wonderful garden conservatory.

Just beyond Marlborough Road, at 1440 Albemarle, you'll see the **J.C. Woodhull House (13)**, a 1905 work by Robert Bryson and Carroll Pratt. This house fuses two styles: Colonial Revival and Queen Anne Revival.

On the opposite side of Albemarle Road, at #1423, is Petit's **Francis M. Crafts House (14)** (1899), which is a beautiful example of the Queen Anne style.

Number 1305 Albemarle Road is the **G. Gale House (15)** (1905), H. B. Moore, architect. It is a Classical Revival design.

Across the street at #1306 you'll see the **John S. Eakins House (16)** (1905), also by Petit. It is a Shingle Style house with a Colonial Revival porch.

By now you should be at the corner of Albemarle and Argyle Roads. Make a right on Argyle and walk one block to Church Avenue. A right on Church Avenue will return you to the starting point of this walk and the subway station.

13 · The Green-Wood Cemetery

Directions: *Take the R or M line to the 25th Street subway station. Walk on 25th Street one block to Fifth Avenue.*

C emeteries as we know them today are a relatively recent innovation. Until the early 1800s most dead were buried in family plots, small burial grounds, or churchyards. That began to change in 1831 when Mount Auburn Cemetery in Cambridge, Massachusetts, was created. It was America's first "garden cemetery." The Green-Wood Cemetery followed in 1838. After the remains of New York governor DeWitt Clinton (1769–1828) were transferred here in 1845, Green-Wood became society's favored burial place. Today over 600,000 bodies are buried in the 478-acre cemetery. These include many notables, among them industrialist and philanthropist Peter Cooper, William "Boss" Tweed, Samuel F. B. Morse, Henry Ward Beecher, and many others, some of whose graves you'll see on this walk.

Leave Fifth Avenue and approach the **Main Entrance Gate (1)** to the cemetery. To say it is a grand entrance would be an understatement. It is a kind of triumphant arch translated into Gothic vocabulary—and inspired by medieval prototypes. Gothic Revival architecture began to bloom in England in the late 18th century and came to full flower in the 19th. One of the champions of the Gothic Revival in America was Richard Upjohn (1802–1878). Upjohn came to America from England in 1829. He lived in Brooklyn (see page 133). At first a carpenter, he later worked as an architect's draftsman. After designing several Gothic villas he drew up plans for Trinity Church, Wall Street. Completed in 1849, Trinity made Upjohn's career and sealed his reputation as one of America's best Goth-

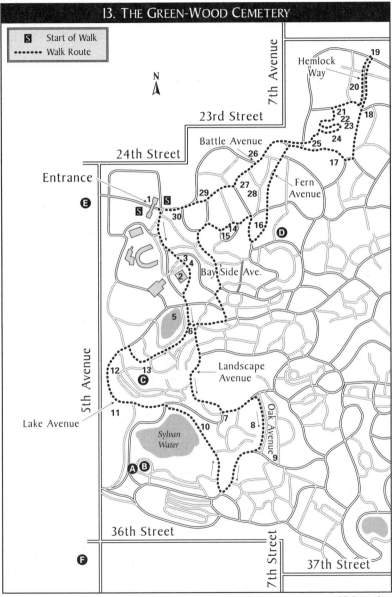

13. THE GREEN-WOOD CEMETERY

S Start of Walk
•••••• Walk Route

N

7th Avenue

23rd Street

24th Street

Entrance

E

Battle Avenue

Hemlock Way

19

20

21
22
23
24

18

25

17

26

29

27
28

Fern Avenue

S
1
S

30

3
4
2

14
15

16

D

Bay Side Ave.

5

6

Landscape Avenue

12   13

C

Lake Avenue

11

7

8

9

Oak Avenue

10

Sylvan Water

A **B**

36th Street

F

37th Street

7th Street

© The Countryman Press

ic Revival architects. He was the first president of the American Institute of Architects.

Upjohn and his son (Richard M. Upjohn) designed the entrance gate and attached gatekeeper's lodge in 1861. The building material they chose is brownstone. Note the traceried gables over the three entryways and the spires, statues, finials, turrets, and crockets above, and the permanent polychrome slate roof over the lodge. The central tower rises 106 feet and houses a funeral bell that tolls to this day. Four reliefs carved from sandstone by the English sculptor John Moffitt are entitled Come Forth, The Dead Shall be Raised, I Am the Resurrection and the Life, and Weep No More. Robert A. M. Stern, dean of the Yale School of Architecture, has said that this entrance gate is America's finest example of High Victorian Gothic architecture.

Enter the gatekeeper's lodge if you like. The Green-Wood Cemetery has a very knowledgeable and courteous staff who will help you with more information. The cemetery's publications are for sale here and there are restroom facilities.

You may hear the sound of many birds when you pass under the arches. Look back at the central pinnacle and you will see a large nest of green monk (or Quaker) parakeets. The first of these birds came from Argentina by airplane, escaped from their cage at John F. Kennedy Airport, and have been happily nesting here ever since.

After entering the cemetery walk to your right. Directly in front of you will be the **Historic Chapel (2)**. Another Gothic Revival work, the chapel was built about 1915. It is modeled on Sir Christopher Wren's Thomas Tower at Christ Church in Oxford, England. The architects here were Warren and Wetmore, best known for designing Grand Central Station. Enter the chapel, rest a bit, and look at its stained glass windows. The limestone chapel was restored in 2000.

When leaving the chapel look to your right to Willow Avenue. What appears to be a small chapel with a double arched entry topped with three squat pinnacles is the **Receiving Tomb (3)**. This receiving tomb (and three more in Manhattan) held the remains of those who died in winter.

Also, the cemetery would allow remains to stay in the receiving tombs for three weeks until a plot was purchased. Another Upjohn design, here he used the Romanesque style. It is set into the side of the hill and ventilated to keep its interior chambers cool. In all, the eight chambers could hold 1,500 bodies.

On the **hillside (4)** behind the receiving tomb you'll see many mausoleums. These reflect some of the many architectural styles popular in the 1800s, most of which were revivals: Egyptian (note the pyramid), Greek, and Romanesque, to name but three.

Willow Avenue will lead you to Landscape Avenue. The pond on your right is **Valley Water (5)**, its fountain recently restored.

Continue your walk on Landscape Avenue. On your right will be the **Tomb of George Catlin (6)** (1796–1872). Catlin was an artist who traveled west and documented American Indian life with countless portraits, village scenes, and the like. Many of his paintings are in the collection of the Smithsonian Institution. He is buried here in the plot owned by his in-laws—the Gregory family. Though he died in 1872, Catlin's grave was not marked with a tombstone until almost 90 years later. It reads: "THIS MONUMENT WAS ERECTED BY THE NEW YORK WESTERNERS AND MEMBERS OF THE CATLIN FAMILY. 1961." His wife Clara is buried a few feet away.

Return to Landscape Avenue and walk until it intersects with Sylvan Avenue on your right. There you will see another Upjohn work: a small Gothic chapel known as the **Browne Mausoleum (7)**. Built in 1843, it is the resting place for the Englishman George W. Browne who was a very successful Manhattan restaurateur.

Landscape Avenue will lead you to Oak Avenue (on your right). Walk on Oak Avenue about 150 feet and on your right you will see a **bust of Horace Greeley (8)** (1811–1872) on the hill. The founder and editor of the *New York Tribune*, Greeley was also an abolitionist and a politician. The pedestal of Greeley's monument displays bronze reliefs illustrating chapters in his life.

On the opposite side of Oak Avenue, about 75 feet up the hill, you will see the winged Angel of Death weeping over the **Cassard tomb (9).** This is a copy of the tomb of the American sculptor William Wetmore Story at Florence, Italy. Unfortunately, the angel has lost its left hand, presumably to vandals.

Follow Oak Avenue to a hairpin turn to the right. You will now be on Lake Avenue. Another pond, Sylvan Water, will be on your left. Opposite the pond is the **grave of Leonard W. Jerome (10)** (1817–1891), Winston Churchill's grandfather. A successful businessman, Jerome owned the *New York Times*. He was also an avid horse breeder and racer. Jerome's family lived at 197 Amity Street in Brooklyn when his daughter Jennie was born (see page 133). Jennie married Lord Randolph Churchill and gave birth to the future prime minister.

Detour A: Make a left on Sylvan Avenue and walk to the opposite side of the pond. On your left will be the round-top tombstone marking the grave of John Thomas Underwood (1857–1937). Underwood lived in Clinton Hill in Brooklyn (see page 140) and his Brooklyn typewriter factory was the world's largest. By the time he died Underwood had manufactured and sold over 5 million typewriters worldwide.

Detour B: To see the graves of the Lorillards, from Sylvan Avenue make a left on Carnation Path and walk to the intersection of Lake Ridge Path. If you stand with your back to Lake Ridge Path, the grave of Peter Lorillard (1763–1843) will be in front of you at number 1. He founded the Lorillard Tobacco Company. Pierre Lorillard IV (1833–1901) lies across the semicircle.

Continue to walk on Lake Avenue. You are reminded that the Green-Wood Cemetery is the burial place of the famous *and* infamous as you walk by the **grave of Albert Anastasia (11)** (1902–1957) on your left. He was the "boss" of a crime syndicate.

Opposite, on your right, the Coney Island entrepreneur **George C. Tilyou (12)** (1862–1914) is buried. Tilyou opened Steeplechase Park in 1897. The park survived him by 50 years, closing in 1964.

Leave Lake Avenue by making a right on Walnut Avenue. Then make a left on Valley Avenue. On your right you'll see a large fanciful Gothic monument over the tomb and effigy of **John Matthews (13)** (1808–

1870). A Liverpool native, Matthews came to New York where he made and sold carbonated drinks. He became known as the "Soda Fountain King." His monument was created by Karl Muller.

Detour C: To see the tomb of David Wesson backtrack on Valley Avenue for about 50 feet. Follow the row of small granite stones on your left for about 125 feet. There you will see a larger monument for David Wesson (1861–1934), the creator of Wesson Oil.

Follow Valley Avenue to Bayside Avenue. Make a left onto Bayside and follow it until it encircles a large oval. There you will see a large bronze **statue of DeWitt Clinton (14)** (1779–1828). A mayor and governor, Clinton's biography and achievements are inscribed on the monument's pedestal. Clinton was first buried at Little Albany Cemetery ten years before the Green-Wood Cemetery existed. The transfer of his body here in 1845 guaranteed the cemetery's legacy as a final resting place for many notables.

The next stop is also on this grassy island. Just a few feet to the right, among hemlock trees, you'll see the **grave of Nathaniel Currier (15)** (1813–1858). He and his partner James Ives (who is also buried in Green-Wood) documented just about every aspect of American life with the thousands of prints they produced. Two Currier and Ives prints are reproduced in this guide on pages 18 and 111.

From the island walk northeast on Bay Side Path. Make a right on Highland Avenue and then make a hairpin turn to the left onto Fern Avenue. On your left take the steps to the **Bennett Family Vault (16)** and note the Italian marble statue of the kneeling woman and child. James Gordon Bennett (1795–1872), founder of the *New York Herald*, is buried here. The site offers fine views of Manhattan. Continue your walk north on Fern Avenue.

Detour D: To see two monuments of exceptional artistic merit, make a right on Atlantic Avenue and then a right on Hydrangea Path. On your left you'll see the monument to Jane Griffith (1816–1857). Sculpted by Patrizzio Piatti, it depicts Jane standing on the steps of her Manhattan home on the morning of the day she died. She is saying good-bye to her

The Green-Wood Cemetery Main Entrance Gate, stop number 1

ROBERT J. REGALBUTO

husband as he leaves for work. To see the other work, return to Hydrangea Path, turn left, and then make a left onto Fern Avenue. Stop at Greenbough Avenue. On your left is the beautifully carved marble Canda Monument. Charlotte Canda (1828–1845) was accidentally killed when she fell out of a speeding horse carriage. She was 17 and the monument measures 17 feet wide by 17 feet deep and is decorated with 17 rosebuds.

Walk north on Fern Avenue to its end. Then make a right onto Battle Avenue. On your right near Hemlock Avenue is the **bust of Elias Howe (17)** (1819–1867), the Yankee inventor of the sewing machine. The Howes also buried their beloved dog Fannie here in their plot. Be sure to read the epitaph on Fannie's monument.

Make a left on Hemlock Avenue. Just before Garland Avenue there will be **two ginkgo trees (18)** on your right near the tomb of M. Hermann. The ginkgo is an ancient Chinese tree. Be sure not to step on its foul-smelling seeds. If you do, you will understand why, as Brooklyn kids, we would call this the "stinko tree!"

Continue on Hemlock Avenue to its end. Make a right on Border Avenue and on your left is the **grave of Henry Chadwick (19)** (1824–1908). Theodore Roosevelt said Chadwick was the "Father of Baseball." The monument is easy to identify. It is a square column topped with a polished granite ball (perhaps representative of a baseball). The sides of the plinth have baseball emblems: a baseball diamond, crossed bats, a catcher's mask, and a baseball glove. Four granite bases surround the plot. (An interesting aside: Charles Ebbets, who built Ebbets Field, is also buried at Green-Wood.)

Retrace your steps on Hemlock Avenue. On your right, just after Canna Path, lies **Elmer Ambrose Sperry (20)** (1860–1930). One of his many inventions was the gyroscope. He founded a company that became the Sperry Rand Corporation.

Make a right on Garland Avenue. On your left is **Battle Hill (21)** where a part of the Battle of Brooklyn was fought in August 1776. Sixty-two of the battle's casualties were buried here years before Green-Wood was founded. At 216.5 feet, Battle Hill is Brooklyn's highest elevation.

Make a left on Battle Path and climb Battle Hill. On your left you'll see a statue of **Minerva and the Altar to Liberty (22)**. This is a Revolutionary War monument placed here by Charles Higgins. Higgins (who is buried in back of the Minerva monument) owned the Higgins Ink Factory on Ninth Street (see page 85).

Make a left on Liberty Path. On your left is the **grave of Edwin C. Litchfield (23)** (1815–1885). A real estate developer, Litchfield owned much of Park Slope. His home is now the Prospect Park headquarters (see page 85).

Across Liberty Path, on your right, is the **grave of Leonard Bernstein (24)** (1918–1990), a great American composer, conductor, and pianist. Leave a small stone on his tombstone, if you like. It is a Jewish tradition for visitors to a grave to do so.

Return to Battle Path. Turn left. At the end of the path, on the left, you will see the **Soldiers' Monument (25)**. It was placed here in 1869 to honor the 148,000 New Yorkers who fought in the Civil War.

Bear right and continue west on Battle Avenue. On your right you'll see a replica of an **Egyptian Pyramid (26)**. This is the tomb of Albert Ross Parsons (1847–1933), a musician, teacher, and eminent Egyptologist. Parsons wrote a book entitled *New Light from the Great Pyramid.*

Walk farther on Battle Avenue. At the intersection with Highland Avenue ascend the steps to the replica of a **Greek Temple (27)**. The tomb is that of John Anderson (1812–1881) who made his fortune in tobacco. The statues were sculpted by John Moffitt.

To see the **grave of F.A.O. Schwartz (28)** go to the back of Anderson's mausoleum. To your right there will be a row of six granite tombstones, each about 36 inches tall. One of these marks the grave of Frederick Augustus Otto Schwartz (1836–1911) who began his toy-store empire in 1862.

Return to Battle Avenue. Walk south west. On your right, at the corner of Bay View Avenue, you'll see a large **obelisk (29)**. Here are buried 103 of the 278 victims of the Brooklyn Theatre fire that occurred on December 5, 1876.

Just a few steps farther on Battle Avenue beyond Ardon Avenue on your left you'll see the **Stewart mausoleum (30).** Interred here are the parents of Isabella Stewart Gardner. Isabella Stewart married Bostonian John Lowell Gardner. "Mrs. Jack" is best remembered for her cultural contribution to Boston: Fenway Court (or the Isabella Stewart Gardner Museum). This mausoleum is the work of architect Stanford White and sculptor Augustus Saint-Gaudens.

This returns you to the gate and the start of this tour.

Detour E: As you return to Fifth Avenue, on your left you will see New York City's oldest standing greenhouse. A Victorian relic, it was built in 1895 for Weir and Company. It is now owned by McGovern Florist.

Detour F: Do you remember Ralph Kramden of the TV series *The Honeymooners*? The bus driver was portrayed as living in Brooklyn and his buses were dispatched from the Fifth Avenue Bus Depot at 36th Street. To honor the comedian who created the lovable character, the garage was renamed the Jackie Gleason Bus Depot in 1988. Gleason, in real life, was a Brooklynite, too.

14 · Bay Ridge and Fort Hamilton

Directions: *Take the R train to the Bay Ridge Avenue station. Then transfer to the Bay Ridge Avenue bus and get off at Shore Road.*

Bay Ridge was a part of the Dutch town Nieuw Utrecht, which was settled in 1662. For over 200 years this area was called Yellow Hook, which presumably was a reference to the sandy soil here. When yellow fever was epidemic in the 1850s the original name was abandoned. It was the florist James Weir (see page 104) who suggested the name Bay Ridge as this is in fact a ridge overlooking New York Bay. Bay Ridge was dotted with mansions and fashionable country clubs in the late 1800s. The area grew, however, after the subway was extended along Fourth Avenue in 1915. In the early 20th century many Scandinavians lived in Bay Ridge. They were later joined by Italians and Irish. Some parts of Bay Ridge have had stable neighborhoods, many families living there for four generations. Other areas, such as Sunset Park, have seen population shifts over the years and are now home to immigrant groups from diverse places.

The most significant change to Bay Ridge occurred with the building of the Verrazano-Narrows Bridge in the 1960s. The bridge was fiercely opposed by most Bay Ridgers. Many longtime residents were forced to leave their homes in its wake. More of the bridge later on this walk.

A very recent chapter in the history of Bay Ridge was written on August 8, 2007, when a tornado hit 68th and 69th Streets between Third and Fourth Avenues. Eleven houses were destroyed, and many trees were toppled, causing additional damage.

Movies filmed in Bay Ridge include *Saturday Night Fever* (1977), *Out for Justice* (1991), *Brooklyn Rules* (2006), and *What Happens in Vegas* (2008).

14. BAY RIDGE AND FORT HAMILTON

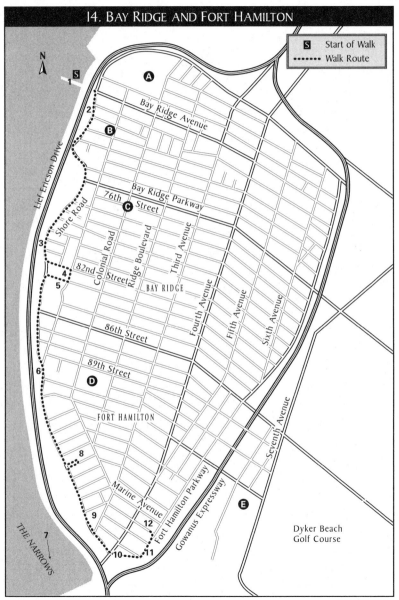

S Start of Walk
••••••• Walk Route

N

1 S

A

Bay Ridge Avenue

2

B

Lief Ericson Drive

Bay Ridge Parkway

76th C Street

Shore Road

Colonial Road

Ridge Boulevard

Third Avenue

3

82nd Street

4

5

BAY RIDGE

Fourth Avenue

Fifth Avenue

Sixth Avenue

86th Street

89th Street

6

D

FORT HAMILTON

Seventh Avenue

8

Marine Avenue

E

9

12

Fort Hamilton Parkway

Gowanus Expressway

Dyker Beach
Golf Course

THE NARROWS

7

10 ••••• 11

© The Countryman Press

Chuck Connors (1921–1992) was from Bay Ridge. He was a professional basketball player (with the Boston Celtics), professional baseball player (with the Brooklyn Dodgers and Chicago Cubs), and an actor with his own TV series (*The Rifleman*). Other local personalities include actor Dan Grimaldi of *The Sopranos* and television anchor Maria Bartiromo. Three Brooklyn Dodgers who lived in Bay Ridge were Duke Snider, Pee Wee Reese (1918–1999), and Carl Erskine.

This is one of the longer walks in this book, but it is also one of the more scenic. Save it for a beautiful day. In preparing this guide I took the walk on a crisp fall evening and I can report to you that the walk was delightful and the sunset was beautiful.

The tour begins at the foot of Bay Ridge Avenue (69th Street) at Shore Road. It continues south along the Narrows—a strait abutted by Staten Island on the west and Brooklyn on the east, connecting Lower and Upper New York Bays. It is also the site of some historic events that we'll recount later.

Start at the **69th Street Pier (1)**. Before Brooklyn and Staten Island were connected by the Verrazano-Narrows Bridge, there was a ferry service from this pier to St. George, Staten Island. The bridge made the Brooklyn ferry redundant and the service was discontinued in 1964. After a period of neglect the pier was restored and is now a place for recreation, fishing, and exercise. It is also a place with outstanding views. A monument beaming a shaft of light into the sky has been placed on the pier as a memorial to the victims of 9/11.

Detour A: Another vantage point nearby is the 27-acre Owl's Head Park, which is perched 100 feet above Shore Road. The entrance is at Colonial Road and Wakeman Place. In the 1800s this was the estate of Henry C. Murphy, the first editor of the newspaper the *Brooklyn Eagle*. He was also a state senator, and a proponent of the Brooklyn Bridge. This later became the home of the Bliss family. And so this is often called Bliss Park. Why is it otherwise known as Owl's Head Park? We're not sure. Perhaps some thought the property is shaped like an owl's head. Yes, there were owls here among the trees. The most likely explanation are

Cannon at the Harbor Defense Museum, stop number 11

the owl's head figures that topped the estate entry gateposts at one time. This became a public park in 1937.

Walk south along Shore Road, which runs parallel with the Belt Parkway (or Leif Ericson Drive in Bay Ridge) and Shore Front Park. Though a public park, it includes the flowers, trees, shrubs, and lily pond of the **Narrows Botanical Garden (2)**, which is privately funded and tended by volunteers.

Detour B: It is a slight detour to the Barkaloo Cemetery at Narrows Avenue and Mackay Place (behind Xaverian High School). It is said to be Brooklyn's oldest cemetery and its only surviving "homestead" burial ground. The property belonged to Jacques Barkaloo (1747–1813). One of his great-granddaughters (Lemma Barkaloo, 1840–1870) was the first American woman to study law.

Detour C: Another detour from Shore Road will bring you to a flight of steps at 76th Street and Colonial Road. The steps lead up to the "ridge" of Bay Ridge. Some say that the flight is reminiscent of San Francisco; others are reminded of the Rue Foyatier at Montmartre in Paris. Putting your imagination aside, if you climb the 61 steps you will be rewarded with the sight of two grand houses: #122 76th Street, which is a Gothic Revival house built about 1900. On the opposite side of 76th Street—at #131— you'll see an 1865 Georgian Revival house with tall portico columns somewhat like those often found on Southern plantation mansions.

Your walk continues on Shore Road. You may want to sit, rest a bit, and enjoy the view from **Old Glory Lookout (3)** between 80th and 81st Streets.

Walk to 83rd Street. Make a left. At the next corner (at 8200 Narrows Avenue) you'll see the **Gingerbread House (4)**. This whimsical cottage with its faux thatched roof and fieldstone chimney was built in 1917 for shipping merchant Howard E. Jones. The architect was J. Sarsfield Kennedy and what he created has been variously described as an Arts and Crafts house, an Art Nouveau design, or even suggestive of a Black Forest house that might have been visited by Hansel and Gretel.

Return to Shore Road and walk by **Fort Hamilton High School (5)**, which was built in 1941 on the site of the exclusive Crescent Athletic Club.

Continue walking south. At 91st Street you'll see the **Michael E. Behlen Circle (6)** with its tidy new gazebo and benches. Those benches offer great views of the **Verrazano-Narrows Bridge (7)**. A few words about "The Verrazano" as locals call it. A bridge spanning the Narrows was proposed in 1926. Thirty-three years later, on August 13, 1959, construction began. It was opened on November 21, 1964, by Mayor Robert F. Wagner. The building cost was more than $320 million. This was the last project headed by Robert Moses, the New York City Parks Commissioner and head of the Triborough Bridge and Tunnel Authority. And it was the last bridge designed by Othmar Ammann who had designed several metropolitan-area spans including the George Washington Bridge.

The bridge's construction was not without opposition. Thousands of Bay Ridge residents had their homes torn down to make a path for it. Historic buildings were demolished. The 19th-century Fort Lafayette, which stood on an island close to Brooklyn, was destroyed; the east tower of the bridge is now anchored on its site.

The Verrazano-Narrows Bridge was the longest suspension bridge in the world for twelve years. In 1981 it was surpassed by England's Humbler Bridge and that in turn was surpassed by Japan's Akashi-Kaikyo Bridge in 1998. The Verrazano, however, remains the largest suspension bridge in the United States. Its span is 4,260 feet and its clearance is 228 feet at mean high water. Many ships are now built to pass under the bridge. The smokestack of the luxury liner *Queen Mary 2*, which docks in New York, was shortened, allowing a clearance of just 9.75 feet.

The height of each tower is 690 feet. They are 4,260 feet distant though their peaks are 1⅝ inches farther apart due to the curvature of the earth. Each tower has 3 million rivets and one million bolts. The suspension cables between the towers each have a diameter of 36 inches, and each cable has 26,108 wires. This totals 143,000 miles of wire.

The Verrazano is a double-decked bridge with six lanes on each level. There have been requests to add both pedestrian walkways and bicycle paths. The annual New York City Marathon begins on the Staten Island end of the bridge and then runs through Brooklyn and the other boroughs, ending in Manhattan.

The Verrazano-Narrows Bridge is now Bay Ridge's most notable landmark and has become a source of pride to many. The bridge is especially beautiful at night when lights on the suspension cables are lit and resemble a string of pearls. It is visible from all five New York boroughs and beyond.

The bridge is at the site where Giovanni da Verrazzano (1485–1528) moored his ship in 1524. Verrazzano, an Italian, was exploring the coast of North America for Francis I, King of France. He first made landfall in South Carolina and then sailed north. He was the first European to enter these waters. From New York the explorer continued north to New England, Nova Scotia, and Newfoundland before setting sail back to Europe. Verrazzano returned to the Western Hemisphere twice. On his last voyage he was killed and devoured by cannibals in the Lesser Antilles.

An 1861 view of the Narrows looking north from Fort Hamilton. Note Fort Lafayette on the left, which was demolished to make way for the eastern tower of the Verrazano-Narrows Bridge.

One final note about the navigator. His name is spelled Verrazzano and the bridge name is spelled Verrazano—minus the second "z."

Venture into the neighborhood at 95th Street. The **Bennet-Farrell House (8)** (private) is at 119 95th Street between Shore Road and Marine Avenue. This Greek Revival house was built on Shore Road in 1847 and was moved here in 1913. The Bennets were descendants of Dutch settlers. James T. Farrell, who bought the house in 1890, was a businessman and a Tammany Hall politician.

Detour D: The Visitation Monastery and Academy occupies the 7-acre block framed by Colonial Road, Ridge Boulevard, 89th Street, and 91st Street. It is on the site of the former Kings County Inebriates' Home. The Visitation nuns bought the property in 1903 and ten years later built the Italian Renaissance chapel. The academy is a primary school for girls run by Roman Catholic cloistered nuns.

Continue south on Shore Road Promenade. **Fontbonne Hall Academy (9)** is at the corner of 99th Street. The academy occupies a former mansion built in 1895 and later bought by the legendary financier Diamond Jim Brady (1856–1917) for his companion, the actress and entertainer Lillian Russell (1860–1922). Subsequently it was used as a casino, a speakeasy, a boys' school, and a private club. Since 1937 it has been a private secondary school for girls. The chapel and other building were later added. Run by the Roman Catholic Sisters of St. Joseph, the school is named for Mother St. John Fontbonne, a member of their congregation who ministered during the French Revolution.

Walk just two more blocks along Shore Road to the **John Paul Jones Park (10).** Jones is called the "Father of the American Navy," immortalized for his words "I have not yet begun to fight." Jones's body was buried in Paris in an obscure cemetery. It was exhumed and brought to America in 1905 aboard the USS *Brooklyn*. He is now interred at the Naval Academy in Annapolis, Maryland. This is also known as Cannonball Park. The large cannon is a Rodman gun—the largest cannon used in the Civil War. It weighs more than 1,000 pounds. This and other similar guns were at Fort Hamilton. The obelisk is inscribed as follows:

> *This Monument*
> *to the*
> *Dover Patrol*
> *erected as a tribute to the*
> *comradeship and service of the*
> *American Naval Forces*
> *in Europe*
> *during the World War*

Sit a while. You are now in the part of Bay Ridge known as Fort Hamilton. It was here that the Lenape Indians had a village they called Nayack. In 1680 Dutch visitors described how the natives lived in longhouses made of bark, each about 60 feet long and 15 feet wide. Seven or eight families lived in one house and each gathered around its own fire for cooking and for warmth. In the waters before you the Lenape Indians rowed their canoes to Verrazzano's ship. It was also from this area that the newly independent Americans fired on British ships on July 4, 1776. Later that summer, on August 23, 16,000 British troops disembarked here. The Battle of Brooklyn followed.

Exit the park at the corner of 101st Street and Fort Hamilton Parkway. There you will see the visitor entrance to **Fort Hamilton and Harbor Defense Museum (11)** (www.harbordefensemuseum.com; 718-630-4349). The museum is closed on Sundays. Adults must have a valid photo identification. Fort Hamilton began as a small battery during the American Revolution. The cornerstone of the fort was laid in 1825 and construction continued for six years. The architect was Simon Bernard who had worked for Napoleon. The fort is named for Alexander Hamilton (1755–1804), first U.S. secretary of the treasury. Captain Robert E. Lee was Fort Hamilton's post engineer from 1841 to 1846, and Lieutenant Thomas "Stonewall" Jackson was also stationed here. Boxing heavyweight champion Sergeant Joe Louis taught boxing at Fort Hamilton in the mid-1940s. Lieutenant Colonel Earl Woods played golf across the road at Dyker Beach Golf Course. His son is Tiger Woods.

The novel *Word of Honor* by Nelson DeMille is set at Fort Hamilton.

The history of the fort is presented at the Harbor Defense Museum. It occupies a *caponier* (or "chicken coup"), which was a small fort built for use as a first line of defense against possible attacks through the fort's gate. This is the only army museum in New York City and displays a collection of military artifacts from the time of the American Revolution through World War II. Visitors may see uniforms, banners, flags, guns, military equipment, and memorabilia, including an 1844 24-pounder flank howitzer. Visitors may learn how to load and fire a 19th-century cannon. There are exhibits on the Battle of Brooklyn. The museum also houses a library and archive that are open by appointment.

Across from the museum is the granite old casemate fort built in 1825–1831. This later became the officers' club. Now known as the Community Club, it is open to the public for lunch and other meals. Call in advance at 718-833-9772.

On leaving Fort Hamilton turn right and walk two blocks to St. John's

Episcopal Church, which is known as the **Church of the Generals (12)** (www.saintjohns1834.org; 718-745-2377). St John's began in 1834. General Robert E. Lee was a member of the parish's vestry 1842–1844. The church register records that General Thomas J. ("Stonewall") Jackson was baptized at St. John's on April 29, 1849. He was 25 years old at the time. NATO commander Matthew B. Ridgeway was a member of this parish. At least eight other generals and an admiral were members of St. John's. The present church was built in 1890 and replaced an earlier Gothic Revival one. Note the sign on the lawn marking the spot where Lee planted a tree in 1841, which was replaced by saplings in 1912 and again in 1935.

This is the end of your walking tour of Bay Ridge. For the nearest subway stop walk up 99th Street. The R train starts at the Bay Ridge station at 95th Street and Fourth Avenue. You'll find a number of places to dine or snack both on Fourth Avenue and on Third Avenue.

Detour E: Poly Prep Country Day School is at 92nd Street and Seventh Avenue. The school is a 25-acre campus with Georgian Revival buildings (built in 1924), trees, ponds, tennis courts, a swimming pool, and all that you'd expect to see at a private prep school. "The Brooklyn Collegiate and Polytechnic Institute" was a boys' school founded in 1854. In 1889 the school split into preparatory and college divisions. This land was bought in 1916 from the Dyker Heights Golf Course. "Poly" became coeducational in the 1970s. Its middle and upper schools (grades 5 through 12) are here; the lower level is at the Henry Hulbert House on Prospect Park West (see page 83).

15 · Coney Island

Directions: *Take the D, F, N, or Q lines to the Coney Island*
Stillwell Avenue subway station.

Coney Island got its name from the Dutch "konijn" (wild rabbits) that once multiplied here. About a century ago Coney Island was connected to the rest of Brooklyn, making this a peninsula rather than an island. "The world's largest playground" is a few blocks' stretch; the rest of the peninsula is residential: Sea Gate, Brighton Beach, and Manhattan Beach.

In the 1800s Coney Island became a resort of large hotels. Things began to change in 1884 when the world's first roller coaster was erected here. It and other thrill rides attracted visitors and the dollar—or rather, the nickel, as Coney Island became known as the "Nickel Empire" when 5 cents could buy a subway ride or a hot dog. Soon Coney Island had large amusement parks like Steeplechase, Luna Park, and Dreamland, as well as hundreds of independently owned rides, sideshows, eateries, and the like. The *WPA Guide to New York City*, written in 1939, describes the scene: "Into Coney proper are crammed rows of flimsy shacks, modern apartment houses, two-story residences, an occasional cottage surrounded by lawns, and a wild array of bathhouses, dance halls, freak shows, fun houses, carrousels, roller coasters, penny arcades, assorted game booths, waxworks, ferris wheels, shooting galleries, souvenir shops, restaurants, tearooms, chop suey parlors, hot dog stands, and custard counters to feed and divert the millions. Two miles of excellent boardwalk, a steamboat pier, two large amusement parks, and a number of famous restaurants maintain the popularity of the resort. Surf Avenue, the main thoroughfare, separates the bazaar from the drab community to

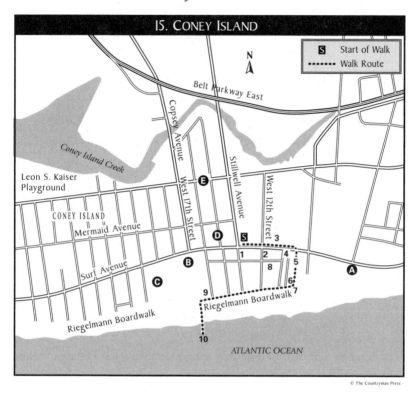

the north where some one hundred thousand persons live the entire year.... Summer crowds are the essence of Coney Island. From early morning, when the first throngs pour from the Stillwell Avenue subway terminal, humanity flows over Coney seeking relief from the heat of the city.... [P]eople of every nationality, boys and girls, feeble ancients, mothers with squirming children, fathers with bundles, push and collide as they rush, laughing, scolding, sweating, for a spot on the sand."

Dreamland burned down in 1911; Luna Park was lost to several fires in the 1940s; Steeplechase closed in 1964. As many Brooklynites lament, "Coney Island ain't what it used to be." However, in 2003 Mayor Michael Bloomberg and others spearheaded the Coney Island Development Corporation. To date $55 million has been appropriated for revitalization.

This tour begins at one of Coney Island's oldest and most enduring establishments: **Nathan's Famous (1)** (www.nathansfamous.com; 718-946-2202). On leaving the subway station walk across Surf Avenue and you'll see Nathan's at the corner of Stillwell Avenue. Nathan's story begins not with a man named Nathan, but rather with a Bavarian immigrant: Charles Feltman. Feltman is credited with creating the "hot dog" by serving a sausage on a long, sliced bun to his customers at his German beer garden. One of his roll splitters was a young man named Nathan Handwerker. In 1916 Handwerker opened his own eatery and undersold Feltman—charging a nickel per hot dog—or half the price of Feltman's dogs. If you love hot dogs you may want to consider entering Nathan's annual hot-dog eating contest on the 4th of July.

From Nathan's Famous make a right on Surf Avenue. On your right at 1208 Surf Avenue (at the corner of West 12th Street) will be **Coney Island USA (2)** (www.coneyislandusa.com; 718-372-5159). Here you'll see the Coney Island Museum. You'll also see "Sideshows by the Sea," the country's only nonprofit freak show. Coney Island USA sponsors the annual Mermaid Parade, which is held the first Saturday of each summer. Coney Island USA is a nonprofit organization founded by Yale graduate Dick Zigun. Have fun.

Just a few steps farther east, on the opposite side of Surf Avenue, you'll see high-rise apartment buildings on the site of **Luna Park (3)**.

Continue on Surf Avenue to West 10th Street. **The Cyclone (4)** roller coaster will be on your right. This is a 1927 "woodie" erected on the site of the world's first roller coater ride (1884). The Cyclone is in Astroland Amusement Park (www.astroland.com; 718-265-2100). The old Feltman's Restaurant was here until it closed in 1946; Astroland was opened in 1954.

Detour A: The Seaside Handball Courts are at Surf Avenue and West Fifth Street. The United States National Handball Association championship games have taken place here.

Next is the **New York Aquarium (5)** at Surf and West 8th (www.nyaquarium.com; 718-265-FISH). There is an admission fee. The first

The author (left) and his brother at Coney Island about 1954. Note the Cyclone in the background.

New York Aquarium opened in 1896 at Castle Garden in Battery Park at the southern tip of Manhattan Island. It closed in 1941, and this aquarium was built in 1955. A wide variety of sea creatures is on view. These include dolphins, beluga whales, penguins, sharks, and electric eels. Children take particular delight in the hands-on experience the Touch-It Tank offers.

Exit to the boardwalk and turn right, proceeding west (toward the Parachute Jump). **Dreamland (6)** stood in the area to your right before it burned down in 1911.

The **Boardwalk (7)** had its first strollers in 1923. Officially the "Edward J. Riegelmann Boardwalk," it honors a Brooklyn borough president. The boardwalk stretches 2.6 miles between Sea Gate and Brighton Beach.

You will see the **Wonder Wheel (8)** on your right in Deno's Amusement Park (www.wonderwheel.com; 718-372-2592). Erected in 1920, it was the creation of Charles Herman. The wheel stands 150 feet tall and weights 200 tons.

Continue your stroll on the boardwalk to another one of Coney Island's enduring legends, "Brooklyn's Eiffel Tower," the **Parachute Jump (9)** (at West 16th Street). This is one of several jumps originally built for military training. It was an attraction at the 1939 New York World's Fair (Flushing Meadow Park, Queens). The Life Savers company sponsored the parachute jump at the fair and so it was painted the same bright colors found on their candy-roll wrappers. After the fair the jump was moved here and was part of Steeplechase Park. Jumpers sat on a bench hanging from a parachute, were lifted up over 200 feet, and then let go on a free fall meant to simulate the fall from an airplane. Though no longer operational, the frame has recently been restored and painted. There are plans underway to floodlight the tower in colors reflecting holidays celebrated (such as red, white, and blue for the 4th of July).

Walk across the boardwalk to **Steeplechase Pier (10)**. The pier juts out 100 feet into the Atlantic Ocean. It's a great place to catch the breeze on a hot summer's evening. Watch out, though, for the fishers casting their lines and hooks.

Detour B: KeySpan Park is at 1904 Surf Avenue between West 17th and West 19th Streets (www.brooklyncyclones.com; 718-449-8497). Steeplechase Park occupied this entire block from 1897 to 1964. KeySpan Park was built in 2001. The cost of the 6,500-seat stadium was $39 million. The Dodgers left Brooklyn in 1957. Brooklyn's baseball team is now the Cyclones, which is a farm team for the New York Mets.

Detour C: The Abe Stark Skating Rink and Convention Hall is at West 19th Street between Surf Avenue and the boardwalk. Abe Stark, "Mr. Brooklyn" to many, was a haberdasher and Brooklyn borough president.

Detour D: Gargiulo's Restaurant is a Brooklyn institution. Located at 2911 West 15th Street between Surf and Mermaid Avenues, Gargiulo's opened in 1907 and has been at this site since 1928 (www.gargiulos.com; 718-266-4891).

Detour E: For those with a lighter appetite, another landmark Coney Island restaurant is Totonno's (1524 Neptune Avenue between West 15th Street and West 16th Street). Totonno's opened in 1924. Its pizza is baked in brick ovens and they have a loyal following who will testify that this is the city's best pizza. But don't plan a late visit. Totonno's will remain open only until they run out of dough!

16 · BAM and Fort Greene

Directions: Take the B, Q, 2, 3, 4, or 5 line to the Atlantic Avenue subway station. Or take the D, M, N, or R train to Atlantic Avenue–Pacific Street station. Another alternative is the Long Island Rail Road to Flatbush Avenue.

Begin at the **Atlantic Terminal Center (1).** A mall housing many stores, this was built in the 1990s by developer Forest City Ratner and at the time of writing the center is being expanded (www.atlanticterminal stores.com). There have been plans to lure the Nets NBA team to Brooklyn by building an arena over the Long Island Rail Road tracks here. The architect chosen is Frank Gehry who designed the much acclaimed Guggenheim Museum in Balboa, Spain.

When you leave the center you'll be facing **Times Plaza (2)** where Atlantic Avenue, Flatbush Avenue, and Fourth Avenue meet. The plaza is named for the now defunct *Brooklyn Times* newspaper that had its editorial offices here. Then, as now, Times Plaza was a meeting point for many mass transit lines, though in times past trolley lines and elevated lines crowded the intersection.

Note the old **IRT Subway Kiosk (3)** on the triangular island in the middle of Flatbush Avenue. It is a 1908 Beaux Arts design by Heins and LaFarge. You'll have to use your imagination to picture the flight of steps that once led from the kiosk connecting the subway below to the "el" above.

Now turn your attention to the towering building in front of you. This is **One Hanson Place (4)** that, when built in 1929, was the Williamsburgh Savings Bank. At 512 feet it is Brooklyn's tallest building. The architects (Halsey, McCormack, and Helmer) thoughtfully embellished the

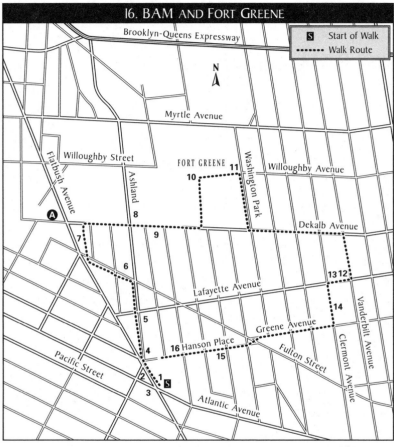

office building with Romanesque and Byzantine details and topped it with a replica of the dome at the original 1870 Williamsburgh Savings Bank building (see page 148). The clocks, each 27 feet in diameter, were the largest in the nation until 1962. No longer a bank and office building, One Hanson Place is now upscale condominiums (www.onehanson.com).

Facing One Hanson Place, walk down Ashland Place and make a right on Lafayette Avenue. You will be at **BAM/Brooklyn Academy of Music (5)** (www.bam.org; 718-636-4100).

Founded in 1859, the academy had a performing arts center on Montague Street in Brooklyn Heights that was destroyed by fire in 1903. This complex was built five years later; Herts and Tallant, architects. BAM went through a period of growth and earned national recognition under the leadership of Harvey Lichtenstein, executive director from 1967 to 1999. The building has been revitalized, including the restoration of the façade's Renaissance Revival cornice and colorful terra cotta. The interior houses an opera house, symphony hall, a multiplex movie theater, and a restaurant.

Return to Ashland Place. Make a right on Ashland and walk north one block to Fulton Street. Make a left on Fulton Street and on your right there is an adjunct of BAM, the **Majestic Theatre (6)** (1903, H. H. Pfeiffer, architect). Now known as the Harvey Lichtenstein Theatre, the "Harvey" presents concerts, plays, and dance performances.

With your back to the Harvey make a right to Rockwell Place. At the corner make another right and walk to 57 Rockwell Place. This is **Urban Glass (7),** a studio where glass artwork is crafted in large kilns. You may watch the artists at work and visit their shop (www.urbanglass.org; 718-625-3685).

From the door of Urban Glass make a right and walk to the next corner. This will be DeKalb Avenue. Baron Johan DeKalb was a Revolutionary War hero who served with Washington and Lafayette.

Detour A: If you're hungry a local restaurant/institution is within walking distance. Junior's is at the corner of DeKalb Avenue and Fulton Street. Opened in 1950, Junior's is known far and wide for its outstanding cheesecake. They also offer a full menu (www.juniorscheesecake.com; 718-852-5257).

Walk east on DeKalb Avenue. Just beyond Ashland Place **Brooklyn Hospital (8)** will be on your left. It dates to 1839.

Walk two more blocks on DeKalb Avenue and **Brooklyn Technical High School (9)** will be on your right at Fort Greene Place. Built in 1931, "Brooklyn Tech" has the transmission tower of WNYE-TV and WNYE-FM. At 591 feet, it is the tallest structure in Brooklyn.

The 30-acre **Fort Greene Park (10)** is on your left. The site of Fort Putnam during the American Revolution, it was renamed in honor of General Nathanael Greene (1742–1786) from Rhode Island. Then in 1847 it was renamed again, this time to Washington Park. Finally, in 1868 Frederick Law Olmsted and Calvert Vaux (the men who created Prospect Park and Central Park) worked their landscaping magic here, too. The name then reverted back to Fort Greene.

The towering Prison Ship Martyrs Monument in the park's center is more than a memorial. It is also a mausoleum. During the American Revolution some 11,000 American soldiers died on British prison ships anchored at Wallabout Bay in the East River. For many years buried on Vinegar Hill (see page 23), their remains were reinterred here in 1873 in a crypt under the stair leading to the pillar. Stanford White was the architect for the monument that was designed in 1906 and dedicated by President William Howard Taft in 1908. Standing 145 feet tall, the Doric column is the world's tallest and is crowned with a brazier, which was lit with a memorial flame.

Bordering the east side of Fort Greene is a street named **Washington Park (11)**. Its brownstones date to the 1860s. This was once one of Brooklyn's most fashionable addresses.

Walk to the corner of Washington Park and DeKalb Avenue. Walk east on DeKalb four short blocks to Vanderbilt Avenue. Make a right on Vanderbilt and, on your right, at the corner of Lafayette Avenue, is **Our Lady Queen of All Saints Church (12)**. The church, school, and rectory were built 1910–1913 when Fr. George Mundelein was pastor. Later he became the cardinal archbishop of Chicago. Gustave Steinbeck designed this in the French Gothic style. The church is reminiscent of the Sainte-Chapelle in Paris.

Make a right on Lafayette Avenue and on your right at the corner of Clermont Street you'll see the **Brooklyn Masonic Temple (13),** built in 1906; Lord and Hewlett, architects.

Now turn left and walk on Clermont one block to Greene Avenue. On the left at 367 Clermont Street is the former **Bishop's Residence (14)**. It

The tower of One Hanson Place, stop number 4

was built in 1887; Patrick C. Keely, architect. The rest of the block is the site of what was to have been one of the largest cathedrals in the world. Construction of the Cathedral of the Immaculate Conception began in 1866 and ended in 1878 due to lack of funds. The cathedral's walls rose 12 feet and a chapel (one of six planned) was completed. These were demolished in 1931 to make way for the Bishop Loughlin Memorial High School that you see today. For years the former bishop's residence housed the brothers teaching at the high school. Today it is a dormitory for the school's minority students participating in the "Anchor Program."

Walk west on Greene Avenue. At Fulton Street jog to the left slightly and continue in the same direction on Hanson Place. Hanson Place was named for Dr. Samuel Hanson Fox (1793–1880), a Presbyterian minister and a founder of the City University of New York. On your left, at the corner of Hanson Place and South Portland Avenue, is the **Hanson Place Seventh-Day Adventist Church (15).** Originally the Hanson Place Baptist Church, it was built 1857–1860 by George Penchard.

Walk three more short blocks on Hanson Place to St. Felix Street. On your right is the **Hanson Place Central United Methodist Church (16)**. It was built in 1929 as was its neighbor, the Williamsburgh Savings Bank. Replacing an earlier 1847 church, the present building is a hybrid, fusing Gothic with Art Moderne.

With this you have come full circle, returning to the Atlantic Terminal Center.

17 · Boerum Hill

Directions: *Take the B, Q, 2, 3, 4, or 5 line to the Atlantic Avenue station. Or take the D, M, N, or R train to Atlantic Avenue–Pacific Street station. Another alternative is the Long Island Rail Road to Flatbush Avenue.*

For 300 years this area was known as North Gowanus as it is near the Gowanus Creek. The creek was developed into an industrial canal in the 1840s. Some think that the creek was named for the Indian sachem Gouwane who sold this land to the Dutch; others say that Gowanus is from the Dutch word *gouwee* or "bay." What is certain is that the neighborhood grew from the 1840s to the 1870s when most of its brownstones and other row houses were built. When gentrification began in the 1970s the neighborhood adopted the name "Boerum Hill" after colonial landowner Simon Boerum.

From Flatbush Avenue walk west on State Street. On your right at 475 State Street is the **Brooklyn Boys' Boarding School (1)**, which dates to 1840. It later became office space for the New York City Board of Education.

Continue your walk on State Street. The houses on your left at **492-496 State Street (2)** are about a century old. They are distinctive in that they are "English row houses"—that is, without stoops (front steps) and have their entrance doors at ground level.

Engine Company 226 (3), New York City Fire Department, is ahead on your right (#409). It dates to 1889. Note the well-preserved decorative cast iron crown at the roofline.

St. Nicholas Antiochian Orthodox Cathedral (4) stands at 355

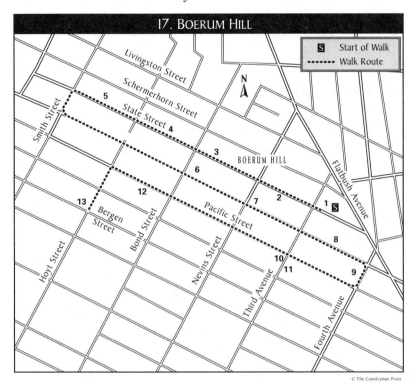

17. BOERUM HILL

S Start of Walk
······· Walk Route

© The Countryman Press

State Street. It is reminiscent of an English country church. The façade is ashlar schist trimmed with sandstone.

Continue your walk on State Street and cross Hoyt Street. Charles Hoyt was a real estate developer who laid out some streets in this area in the 1830s. **State Street between Hoyt and Smith Streets (5)** is lined with Renaissance Revival townhouses that are well maintained. A personal aside: my maternal grandparents lived on this block about 100 years ago. Poles, they left their home in the Austro-Hungarian Empire, passed through Ellis Island, and settled on State Street.

Make a left on Smith Street and then a left again onto Atlantic Avenue. Walk down Atlantic Avenue and browse though its many antique shops and Middle Eastern stores. The **Byelorussian Autocephalic Orthodox**

Church (6) is just across Bond Street on your left, and the **House of the Lord Pentecostal Church (7)** is also on your left beyond Nevins Street. The former is Gothic; the later is Late Romanesque Revival. Nevins Street was named for another real estate developer, Russell H. Nevins. Nevins and Hoyt were business partners.

Farther along Atlantic Avenue, just beyond Third Avenue, you'll see a cheerful cluster of shops on your left. Collectively these form **Atlantic Gardens (8)**. The gardens are in back of the stores. Note the glazed terra cotta on the building across the avenue at numbers 552-554.

Make a right on Fourth Avenue. At the corner of Fourth Avenue and Pacific Street is my favorite building on this tour: the **Church of the Redeemer (9)**. Though an Episcopal church, it is the work of Brooklyn architect Patrick C. Keely who designed hundreds of Roman Catholic churches. This Gothic Revival gem was built in 1870. Later a World War I memorial was added: St. Thomas Chapel. At 6 feet square, it may be the smallest chapel in the world. Its interior walls contain stones from Canterbury Cathedral. Good things come in small packages.

Walk down Pacific Street. The **Swedish Evangelical Bethlehem Lutheran Church (10)** will be on your left at the corner of Third Avenue. It was built in 1894. At that time many Swedes lived in this area and Atlantic Avenue was known as the "Swedish Broadway."

From Pacific Street make a left on Third Avenue and on your left will be the former **New York Times Brooklyn Printing Plant (11)** (1929).

Return to Pacific Street and resume your walk westerly. Walk two blocks and cross Bond Street. Stop at **374 Pacific Street (12)** on your left. This is a Gothic Revival house, which is unusual since most Gothic Revival buildings are churches or schools. Two neighboring houses of note are #360, a wooden house dating to 1860, and #358, a former chapel now used as an artist's studio.

Make a left on Hoyt Street and walk two short blocks to Bergen Street, which gets its name from Bergen, Norway. A ship's carpenter who once lived in Bergen settled here. Stop at 148 Hoyt Street at the corner of Bergen. This is the former **Boerum Hill Café (13).** The café was one of several speakeasies that dotted the neighborhood during prohibition.

This is where your tour of Boerum Hill ends. The nearest subway station is one block away at Smith Street (the Bergen Street station where the F and G lines stop). Or you may want to amble back to Fourth Avenue on Dean Street, viewing its handsome row houses along the way.

18 · Cobble Hill

Directions: *Take the 2, 3, 4, or 5 train to Borough Hall. Alternately, take the M or B lines to Court Street. A third option is the Jay Street Borough Hall station where the A, C, and F lines stop.*

The Dutch settlers called this area *ponkiesbergh*, which the English translated as Cobble Hill—a reference to the ships' ballast stones once tossed here. During the American Revolution George Washington was at Cobble Hill Fort for a part of the Battle of Brooklyn. In the 1840s and 1850s this was a fashionable neighborhood. By the 1950s it had become the poor man's Brooklyn Heights. The name Cobble Hill was forgotten and the neighborhood lost its identity. It simply became a part of "South Brooklyn." The name Cobble Hill was used again in the 1960s when the neighborhood began a process of revitalization.

From Borough Hall walk south on Court Street to Atlantic Avenue. Atlantic Avenue itself is a worthwhile walk. There is a large Arab community here, and Atlantic Avenue is its "Main Street" with shops, grocers, and restaurants that cater to Middle Eastern clientele. As an example, Sahadi's Gourmet Emporium (718-624-4550) at 187 Atlantic Avenue has been in business for over 50 years. Close by, at 195 Atlantic Avenue, is the Damascus Bakery. Atlantic Avenue also has many antique shops.

Hidden beneath Atlantic Avenue there is a **railroad tunnel (1)** that was in use between 1844 and 1859. It ran below Atlantic Avenue from the waterfront where ferries arrived. Passengers were met there by steam trains run by the Brooklyn Central and Jamaica Railroad (a forerunner of today's Long Island Rail Road). When the steam train was outlawed in Brooklyn in 1861 the half-mile-long tunnel was sealed. In 1980 historian and railroad buff Bob Diamond was able to locate and access it, and today the

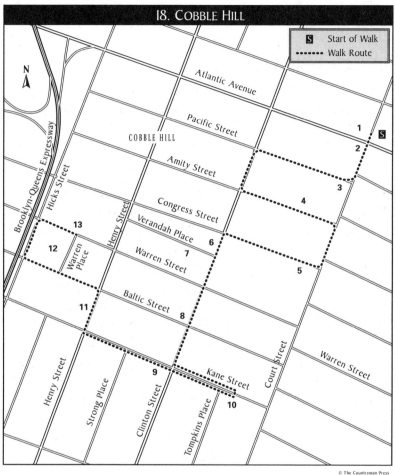

18. COBBLE HILL

S Start of Walk
•••••• Walk Route

N

Atlantic Avenue

Pacific Street

COBBLE HILL

Amity Street

Brooklyn-Queens Expressway

Hicks Street

Henry Street

Congress Street

Verandah Place

Warren Place

Warren Street

Baltic Street

Heny Street

Strong Place

Clinton Street

Tompkins Place

Kane Street

Court Street

Warren Street

1
2
3
4
5
6
7
8
9
10
11
12
13

© The Countryman Press

Brooklyn Historic Railway Association offers scheduled tours through the brick-arched tunnel (www.brooklynrail.net/about_aatunnel.html; 718-941-3160).

The building at **130 Court Street (2)** (at the corner of Atlantic Avenue) may look like an Italian palazzo, but it was a bank for many years and is now a Trader Joe's. This was built in 1922 by architects McKenzie, Voorhees, and Gmelin. Note the cornice up above which is supported by many eagles. Here you'll also see a bronze plaque on the façade reminding passersby that George Washington had his headquarters here during the Battle of Brooklyn.

Walk down Court Street one block and make a right on Pacific Street. On your left, at #174, you'll see the former **Public School #78 (3)** (1889). Today this is an apartment building.

At the next corner make a left onto Clinton Street and then another left onto Amity Street. Stop at **197 Amity Street (4)**. It was in this house that Winston Churchill's mother was born on January 9, 1854. Her name was Jennie Jerome. In 1874 she married Lord Randolph Churchill and the rest is history. Jennie's father, Leonard Jerome, is buried in the Green-Wood Cemetery (see page 99).

Make a right on Court Street and another right on Congress Street. Before you is **St. Paul's, St. Peter's, Our Lady of Pilar Church (5)**. It is an 1838 work of Gamaliel King who also designed Brooklyn City Hall (now Borough Hall). The copper steeple was added in the 1860s.

Walk to Clinton Street. Cross the street and have a seat on a bench in **Cobble Hill Park (6)**. There was a church on the site of this park: Second Unitarian Church. It stood here from 1858 until it was demolished a century later. It was also known as the "Church of the Holy Turtle" because its low, wide dome resembled a turtle's shell. The Rev. Samuel Longfellow, brother of the famous American poet, was the first minister at the church.

Facing the park with your back to Clinton Street, Verandah Place will be on your left. The **Thomas Wolfe House (7)** is a stone's throw away at 40 Verandah Place. The great American novelist rented an apartment here for a time.

And now to go from the home of a great writer to the home of a great architect. On leaving Verandah Place make a right on Clinton Street. Number 296 Clinton Street is the **Richard Upjohn House (8)**. Upjohn, born in England, settled in Brooklyn and became the prolific designer of Gothic Revival churches and houses. His best known works are Trinity Church, Wall Street and the gate to the Green-Wood Cemetery. He was

Thomas Wolfe House, 40 Verandah Place, stop number 7

also the first president of the American Institute of Architects. This house was built in 1843 and Upjohn's son Richard M., also an architect, made an addition to it fifty years later.

Resume your walk south on Clinton Street. At the next corner you will see the lofty 117-foot-high tower of **Christ Church (9)**(Episcopal), designed by (you guessed it) Richard Upjohn. Appropriately, it is an English Gothic design. Its walls are ashlar brownstone and various shades of sandstone. The church was completed in 1841 and many of its furnishings—stained glass windows, altar, altar screen, communion rail, lectern, pulpit, and chairs—were supplied by Louis Comfort Tiffany in 1917. Unfortunately some Tiffany windows were lost in a 1939 blaze.

Cross Clinton Street and walk down Kane Street. The **Kane Street Synagogue (10)** (Congregation Baith Israel Anshei Emes) will be on your right. Dating to 1856, this is "Brooklyn's oldest Jewish congregation that still serves the community in which it was founded." The building also dates to 1856 and at first was the Middle Dutch Reformed Church. It later became the Trinity Lutheran Church before becoming a synagogue. Now faced with stucco, the Romanesque Revival building was once brownstone and brick. The great American composer Aaron Copland (1900–1990) celebrated his bar mitzvah here in 1913.

Retrace your steps on Kane Street and walk as far as Henry Street. Make a right on Henry Street. The **F. A. O. Schwartz Houses (11)** are numbers 412, 414, and 416 Henry Street. The Austrian immigrant, who made his fortune in toys, owned these three houses.

Make a left on Baltic Street. The **Home Buildings (12)** at 134-140 Baltic Street and those around the corner at 439-445 Hicks Street were built in 1877 for Brooklyn philanthropist Alfred Treadway White. White was the first man in America to build low-rent housing. The Workingmen's Cottages that line Warren Place between Baltic and Warren Streets were a part of the same project. There are 34 cottages and 226 apartments in the complex.

Next is **St. Peter's, Our Lady of Pilar Church (13)** on Warren Street between Hicks and Henry Streets. It is an 1860 work of Patrick C. Keely, another Gothic church architect who was based in Brooklyn. Adjacent are the former St. Peter's Academy (1866) and the former St. Peter's Hospital (1888), which is now the Cobble Hill Health Center.

19 · Carroll Gardens

Directions: *Take the F or G train to the Carroll Street subway station.*

We may thank Richard Butts for Carroll Gardens. When he planned the neighborhood in 1846 he had the foresight to add yards *in front* of the row houses. Ever since the residents have cultivated these as gardens.

Through most of the 20th century Carroll Gardens was a largely Italian neighborhood and remains so today. For many years it was simply a part of "South Brooklyn." The naming of "Carroll Gardens" in the 1960s was a clever move, referencing Carroll Street and the many garden-fronted houses here. The name paints a pleasant picture in the mind's eye; it also gives the neighborhood definition and distinction.

Who was Carroll? Charles Carroll of Maryland came from a wealthy family; he had an estate of 80,000 acres. He was the only Roman Catholic to sign the Declaration of Independence, and the last signer to die (in 1832 at the age of 95). Carroll has a Brooklyn connection: he strongly advocated sending Maryland troops here to fight the British in what became the Battle of Brooklyn in August 1776.

For you movie fans: Cher and Nicholas Cage were filmed here in some scenes for *Moonstruck* (1987).

From the subway station walk one block west on First Place to Court Street. Look to your left. At the southwest corner of the intersection is **98 First Place (1)**. This is a brownstone house that dates to about 1860. It is Italianate in style, incorporating features often found in Italian farmhouses: round-top windows, low sloping roofs, and large overhanging eaves supported by decorative pediments.

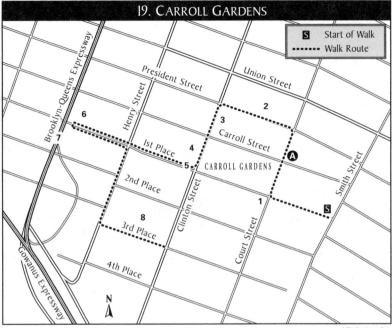

19. CARROLL GARDENS

Brooklyn-Queens Expressway

President Street

Union Street

Henry Street

S — Start of Walk
••••• — Walk Route

6

7

3

Carroll Street

2

1st Place

4

5 CARROLL GARDENS

A

2nd Place

Clinton Street

Smith Street

1

8

3rd Place

Court Street

S

4th Place

Gowanus Expressway

N

© The Countryman Press

Make a right on Court Street and walk two blocks to President Street. Note the large Romanesque church building on the corner. This is the former **South Congregational Church (2)** (1857) and chapel (1851). Both church and chapel are now apartments. Just next door (that is, to the west of Court Street) is the church's Ladies' Parlor. It was designed by F. Charles Merry in 1889. The parlor is now used for church services. The rectory at 255 President Street (an 1895 Woodruff Leeming work) completes the group.

Continue to walk down President Street to Clinton Street, an avenue named for New York governor DeWitt Clinton (1769-1828). Make a left on Clinton Street. On your left will be **St. Paul's Church (3)** (www .stpaulscarrollst.org; 718-625-4126). This Episcopal church was designed by Richard Upjohn and his son Richard M. Upjohn. The elder Upjohn designed many Gothic Revival churches, the best known being Trinity

John Rankin House, stop number 4

Church at the foot of Manhattan's Wall Street. The dark brown sandstone church was built between 1867–1884. Never completed, St. Paul's was to have a towering steeple. This is an "Anglo-Catholic" parish where traditional services, solemn high mass, the use of incense, musical excellence, and Elizabeth English are presented and cherished.

Diagonally across the intersection is the **John Rankin House (4)** at 440 Clinton Street. This mansion is a pristine example of a Greek Revival house. When it was built in 1840, this brick and granite house stood surrounded by fields and farmland and had unobstructed views of Upper New York Bay. Beautifully preserved, the house is still a residence. It is also in use as the F. G. Guido Funeral Home.

Walk south one more block to 450 Clinton Street. This brownstone building was built about 1865 as the **Westminster Presbyterian Church**

(5). In 1929 this became the Den Norske Sjomannskirke (or Norwegian Seamen's Church). The Norwegian seamen have sailed on, and this is now an apartment building. Its architectural style is best described as "eclectic."

Make a right on First Place and walk two blocks to **Sacred Hearts of Jesus and Mary and St. Stephen's Church (6)**. This Roman Catholic church was designed by Patrick C. Keely, a Brooklyn architect responsible for about 700 churches across America. This church (formerly St. Stephen's) is the heart of the Italian-American community that surrounds it.

Across the street is the **Brooklyn-Queens Expressway (7)**, which cut off Red Hook from Carroll Gardens when constructed in 1957.

Retrace your steps to Henry Street. Make a right on Henry Street and walk two blocks to Third Place. Make a left on Third Place and on your left at **numbers 37-39 Third Place (8)** you will see a pair of 1875 houses. Note the mansard roofs and the cast iron decorative grills crowning them.

Third Place will lead you back to Court Street and beyond that to Smith Street where this walk began.

Detour A: If you're looking for a quick bite to eat try Leonardo's Brick Oven Pizza at 383 Court Street (at First Place). It is said that Leonardo serves the best pizza in the neighborhood, and that's saying a lot (718-624-9620).

Not in the mood for pizza? Try Joe's Luncheonette at 349 Court Street (between Union and President Streets) (718-625-3223).

For a more formal setting there's Marco Polo Restaurant at 345 Court Street (at the corner of Union Street) (718-852-5015). It has the reputation of being one of Brooklyn's best Italian restaurants.

Red Rose Restaurant (315 Smith Street between President and Union) is closer to the subway station (718-625-0963). It's another favorite with the locals.

20 · Clinton Hill

Directions: Take the G train to the Clinton-Washington Avenue subway station.

The namesake of Clinton Hill is Governor DeWitt Clinton (1769–1828). Clinton Hill and adjoining Fort Greene were collectively known as "The Hill" in the late 19th century when the Pratts (of the Standard Oil Company), the Bristols (of Bristol-Myers Pharmaceuticals), the Underwoods (of typewriter fame), and other industrial barons built their mansions here—some of which you will see on this walk.

Exit the subway station at the corner of Lafayette Avenue and Washington Avenue. **Underwood Park (1)** is on the northwest corner of the intersection. This is the site of the mansion of John T. Underwood, who amassed a fortune in the manufacture of typewriters worldwide. In his will Underwood directed that he wanted his mansion demolished and the property given to the city for use as a public park.

Walk north on Washington Avenue. The former **Graham Home for Old Ladies (2)** will be on your left at #320. The home was a joint effort of Underwood (who donated the property) and paint manufacturer John B. Graham (who paid for the building of this Romanesque Revival building). The home dates to 1851 and was run under the auspices of the Brooklyn Society for the Relief of Respectable Aged Indigent Females.

Retrace your steps to Lafayette Avenue. Make a left on Lafayette to St. James Place. On your left will be **Emmanuel Baptist Church (3)**. A Francis H. Kimball work, it dates to 1887. The massive yellow Ohio sandstone façade of this church recalls 13th-century French Gothic cathedrals.

Make a left on St. James Place and walk one block to **Pratt Institute (4)**, which was founded in 1887 by Charles Pratt. Pratt made his fortune

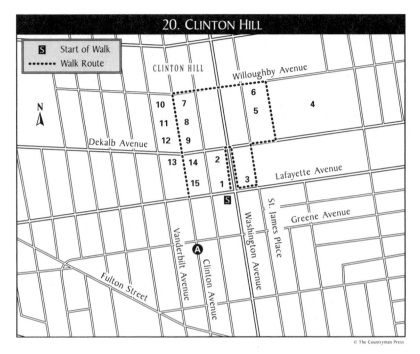

20. CLINTON HILL

S Start of Walk
••••••• Walk Route

CLINTON HILL

Willoughby Avenue

N

Dekalb Avenue

Lafayette Avenue

Greene Avenue

St. James Place

Washington Avenue

Vanderbilt Avenue

Clinton Avenue

Fulton Street

© The Countryman Press

in oil and was one of nine participants with John D. Rockefeller in the Standard Oil Trust. Pratt did not have a college degree and wanted others to have the opportunity for a formal education. Today Pratt Institute is the second largest independent college of art, design, and architecture in the United States, and the largest in the Northeast. The campus is 25 landscaped acres in Clinton Hill. Pratt also has a satellite campus on 14th Street in Manhattan.

Enter the campus on De Kalb Avenue just east of St. James Place. Ryerson Walk will lead you across the Sculpture Park on a campus dotted with 50 works by Pratt students, alumni, faculty, and other artists. On your left is the **Library (5).** The brick Romanesque Revival building was the 1896 work of William B. Tubby. This was Brooklyn's first free public library and the gift of Charles Pratt. In 1940 this ceased to be a public library and is now solely for use by the institute.

Take a few more paces on Ryerson Walk and the **Rose Garden (6)** will be on your left.

Exit the campus at Willoughby Avenue. Make a left and walk three short blocks to Clinton Avenue. Make another left onto Clinton. It was on this block that Charles Pratt built his mansion and three more for his sons. Start at the **Caroline Ladd Pratt House (7)**, which is on your left at #229. The elder Pratt built this for his son Frederick B. in 1895; Babb, Cook, and Willard, architects. It combines Renaissance and Georgian Revival styles. Today this is the official residence for the president of Pratt Institute.

Next is the **Charles Millard Pratt House (8)** at #241. This 1890 Richardsonian Romanesque house was built for Charles Pratt's eldest son. The architect was William B. Tubby, who also designed the library seen earlier on this walk. Today this is the official residence of the Bishop of the Roman Catholic Diocese of Brooklyn.

The **George DuPont Pratt House (9)** is a couple of steps away at #245. Very English and very Georgian, it is now a part of St. Joseph's College. It is another Babb, Cook, and Willard house (1901).

Another trio of mansions stands across the street. St. Joseph's College also owns the **Charles Pratt House (10)** at #232. The Pratt family patriarch had this house built in 1875; the others followed. The architect for this Italianate brownstone house was Ebenezer L. Roberts.

The **Behrend H. Huttman House (11)** is next at #278. It was built in 1884. Note its Baroque details.

The **William W. Crane House (12)** stands at #284. An earlier work, this is a Stick Style house designed by Field and Correja in 1854.

Continue your walk south on Clinton Avenue and cross DeKalb Avenue. Houses of note include the **William Harkness House (13)** (1889) at #300, and the **John Arbuckle House (14)** (1888) at #315. Arbuckle accumulated a fortune with the sale of Yuban Coffee. The **James H. Lounsberry House (15)** is the brownstone mansion at #321. It dates to 1875.

Library, Pratt Institute, stop number 5

Detour A: The parade of mansions continues on Clinton Avenue below Greene Avenue. The Church of St. Luke and St. Matthew (Episcopal) is at 520 Clinton Avenue between Fulton Street and Atlantic Avenue. It is the work of Brooklyn architect John Welsh and was built 1888–1891. It is essentially a Romanesque Revival church embellished with Gothic details. Note the varying shades of brownstone used.

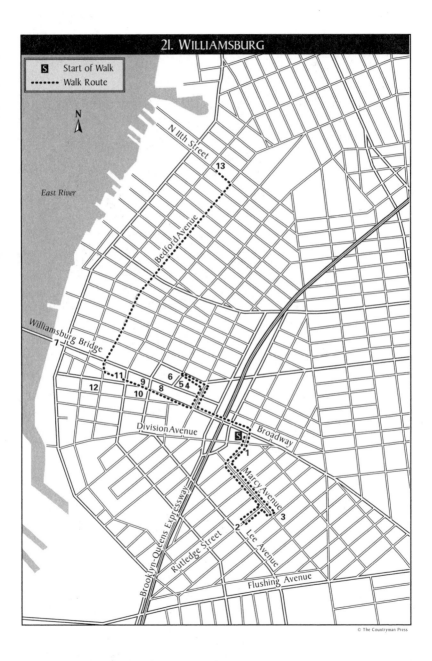

21. WILLIAMSBURG

S Start of Walk
•••••• Walk Route

N

East River

Williamsburg Bridge

N 11th Street

Bedford Avenue

13

7

11
12   9
10   8   6
5 4

Division Avenue

Broadway

S

1

Marcy Avenue

Lee Avenue

2   3

Brooklyn-Queens Expressway

Rutledge Street

Flushing Avenue

© The Countryman Press

21 · Williamsburg

Directions: Take the J, M, or Z train to the Marcy Avenue elevated MTA stop.

The first Europeans to settle here in the 1600s were Dutch, Scandinavian, and French farmers. In 1810 Colonel Jonathan Williams—a grandnephew of Benjamin Franklin—surveyed the area that was later named for him: Williamsburgh. In the 19th century Williamsburgh became a resort for "Commodore" Cornelius Vanderbilt and other industrial barons. Some wealthy businessmen built mansions and banks here—some of which you will see on this tour. Curiously, when Williamsburgh joined the city of Brooklyn in 1855 the "h" was dropped from its name.

Industry came to Williamsburg in the form of breweries (Schaefer Beer and Rheingold Beer), sugar refineries (Domino Sugar), the Pfizer Pharmaceutical Company, and oil refineries (including Charles Pratt's Astral Oil Works, which later partnered with the Standard Oil Company). At first Williamsburg's Germans, Austrians, and Irish worked in its plants. With the opening of the Williamsburg Bridge in 1903, Italians, Poles, Russians, and Jews crossed the bridge, escaping the crowded conditions of Manhattan's Lower East Side. Williamsburg's Hasidic Jewish community has grown to number 50,000 today. After World War II Puerto Ricans and other Hispanics moved into Los Sures—or Southside—of Williamsburg. The Northside has recently experienced an influx of artists and young professionals who share the neighborhood with Poles and Italians.

The novel *A Tree Grows in Brooklyn* is set in Williamsburg. It was written by local author Betty Smith in 1943. The novel was made into an Oscar-winning film in 1945. It was also adapted as a play and a musical.

Comedian Mel Brooks, singer Barry Manilow, and TV personality Geraldo Rivera were all raised in Williamsburg.

An annual event in Williamsburg is Giglio Sunday. Sponsored by Our Lady of Mount Carmel Church, this Italian feast runs for two weeks and culminates with a parade of the *Giglio*: a 65-foot-high tower on which dozens of paper mache angels, saints, and other figures are perched. The feast takes place in July (www.olmcfeast.com; 718-384-0223).

This tour begins in Hasidic Williamsburg. The walk will then move on to the Williamsburg's "bohemia"—the Northside with its trendy shops, hip eateries, and art galleries.

A fun (and healthy) way to start your tour is by walking across the Williamsburg Bridge. An alternative is to take the J, M, or Z line to the Marcy Avenue "el" station. On the train you will also approach Williamsburg on the bridge. After leaving the train the descent to Broadway is a dramatic introduction to Hasidic Williamsburg.

Walk east on Broadway past its many stores overshadowed (literally) by the el. Make a right on Keap Street. At 274 Keap Street (between Marcy Avenue and Division Avenue) is **Bnos Yakov of Pupa (1)**. Built in 1876, this originally was the Temple Beth Elohim—the first Hebrew congregation in Williamsburg, dating to the 1850s. Today this a temple of the Pupa Hasidim. *Bnos Yakov* is translated as "Daughters of Jacob." Pupa is a town in Hungary in which many Orthodox rabbis were educated. The building has many High Victorian Gothic features in the manner of John Ruskin. These include the permanent polychrome of the bricks and stonework, decorative tiles, terra cotta, and stained glass.

Continue on Keap Street to the next corner and make a left on Marcy Avenue. Walk four short blocks on Marcy Avenue and then make a right on **Rutledge Street (2)**. Rutledge between Marcy and Lee is in the heart of Hasidic Williamsburg and it is one of its most attractive residential streets.

Return to Marcy Avenue. Make a right and walk one block on Marcy to the corner of Heywood. The **17th Corps Artillery Armory (3)** (formerly the 47th Regiment Armory) dates to 1883. Before the armory was

The Williamsburgh Savings Bank, stop number 9

built this was the Union Grounds where baseball was played in the 1860s by teams such as the Brooklyn Eckfords, New York Mutuals, the Cincinnati Red Stockings, and the Philadelphia Athletics. More recently the armory has been used as a studio for Robert De Niro's Tribeca Film Company.

Retrace your steps to Broadway. Walk past the el stop to Havemeyer Street. Make a right on Havemeyer and before you is **Washington Plaza (4)**. The equestrian **Statue of George Washington (5)** depicts our first president at Valley Forge. It was modeled by Henry M. Shrady in 1906.

On your right (at the corner of South Fifth Street and New Street) is **Holy Trinity Church (6)** of the Ukrainian Autocephalic Orthodox Church. This was built in 1906 as the Williamsburg Trust Company by architects Helmle and Huberty. The façade is faced with terra cotta.

Return to Broadway and walk toward the **Williamsburg Bridge (7).** When it was constructed in 1903 it had the distinction of being the first bridge with steel towers and the bridge with the longest span. It was designed by Leffert L. Buck. The Williamsburg Bridge was needed to relieve the congestion on the Brooklyn Bridge, which was built twenty years earlier.

The dark building on your right at 195 Broadway is cast iron. Built in 1882, it was the **Sparrow Shoe Factory Warehouse (8)**.

Next on your right is the **Williamsburgh Savings Bank (9)** at 195 Broadway. This magnificent Renaissance Revival work was designed by George B. Post in 1870. Its massive dome was reproduced on top of the Williamsburgh Savings Bank Tower in 1929 (see page 122).

The bank faces another great Williamsburg institution: **Peter Luger Steak House (10)** at 178 Broadway. The restaurant has been in operation since 1887. The décor and atmosphere are reminiscent of a German beer hall with dark paneling, tin ceilings, and sawdust-covered floors. The steaks here are said to be the very best available, which may justify the exorbitant prices. Cash only (www.peterluger.com/Brooklyn;718-387-7400).

Take a few paces further along Broadway. On your right will be the

Williamsburg Art & Historical Center (WAH) (11) at #135 (www.wah center.net; 718-486-7372). This Second Empire edifice was built in 1868 to house the Kings County Savings Bank. The architects were King and Wilcox. Its original gas light fixtures and interior details are well preserved. Restored in 1996, WAH is now galleries and a place for performances, films, lectures, and talks.

Across Broadway (at 134-136) there's another former bank. This was the **Nassau Trust Company (12)**. A Renaissance Revival work, its exterior is limestone and granite. Frank J. Helmle was the architect.

From Broadway make a right onto Bedford Avenue and walk north a few blocks. You'll see that Bedford Avenue and the next street parallel to it, Berry Street, have many art galleries, restaurants, and shops.

If you'd like to rest your feet a bit, you have the option of taking the M61 bus on Bedford Avenue.

The next stop on this tour is the **Brooklyn Brewery (13)** at 79 North 11th Street (www.brooklynbrewery.com; 718-486-7422). Walk (or ride) on Bedford Avenue to 11th Street. Make a left on 11th Street. The brewery will be the yellow building on your right.

About 100 years ago there were perhaps 50 breweries in Brooklyn. The last of these—Rheingold and Schaefer—brewed their final kegs in 1976. Now Williamsburg has the Brooklyn Brewery. Occupying an 1860s steel foundry since 1996, Brooklyn Brewery is now one of the nation's top thirty breweries. Tours are given on Saturdays; the tasting room is open Friday evenings. The Brewhouse gift shop is here also.

This is where this walk ends. The nearest subway stop is the Bedford Avenue station at Bedford and North Seventh Street (on the L line). If you're hungry there are a number of eateries on Bedford Avenue and Berry Avenue. Some are ethnic; others are artsy/chic. Bon appetit!

22 · Greenpoint

Directions: *Take the G train to Greenpoint Avenue station.*

Greenpoint was very verdant when the Europeans arrived in the 1600s. A shipbuilding center in the 19th century, the ironclad ship *Monitor* was built and launched in here to do battle in the Civil War. Greenpoint and neighboring Williamsburg became a center for the "five black arts"—printing, the making of iron, glass, and pottery, and the refining of oil and gas. The workforce and population were immigrants from Poland, Russia, Italy, and Ireland. The wave of immigration continues today as thousands of Poles settle in Greenpoint joining the more than 200,000 fellow Polish-Americans already resident here. For Poland's first free election in 1990, more than 5,000 absentee ballots were mailed from Greenpoint. The Polish presence will be obvious as you walk on this tour. You will see Polish restaurants, bakeries, shops, travel agencies, law offices, and the like.

Greenpoint's most famous daughter is the actress Mae West (1893–1980).

It is said that "Brooklynese" has its roots in Greenpoint. For the unfamiliar, Brooklynese is a dying language in which "these, those, and thems" becomes "deese, dose, 'n' dems" and "oil" is pronounced "earl." Some would call this "the king's English," which may be accurate since Brooklyn is, in fact, in Kings County!

When you exit the subway you'll be at the corner of Greenpoint and Manhattan Avenues. Walk north on Manhattan Avenue just one block to Kent Street. Kent Street is named for the judge and scholar James Kent (1763–1849). Make a left on Kent Street and on your right will be **St. Elias Greek Rite Catholic Church (1)**. Built in 1869–1870, this was

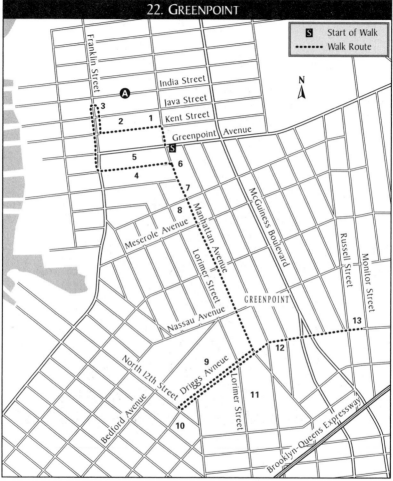

22. GREENPOINT

S Start of Walk
••••••• Walk Route

Franklin Street

India Street
Java Street
Kent Street
Greenpoint Avenue

A

3
2   1

S

5   6
4   7
8

Meserole Avenue

McGuiness Boulevard

Manhattan Avenue

Lorimer Street

Russell Street

Monitor Street

GREENPOINT

Nassau Avenue

13
12

North 12th Street

Driggs Avenue

9

Lorimer Street

11

Bedford Avenue

10

Brooklyn-Queens Expressway

N

© The Countryman Press

originally the Reformed Dutch Church of Greenpoint. The architect was William B. Ditmars, and this High Victorian Gothic church was heavily influenced by the architectural historian John Ruskin who advocated the use of various colors of stonework and brick, thereby creating a "permanent polychrome." The Sunday School building is eight-sided. Octagonal houses and other buildings were very much in vogue in the 1850s–70s.

ROBERT J. REGALBUTO

The Russian Orthodox Cathedral of the Transfiguration of Our Lord, stop number 10

Just a few steps further along Kent Street there is another church: the **Church of the Ascension (2)** (Episcopal), which looks very much like an English village church.

Note the row of townhouses across the street that date to the 1860s.

At the next corner make a right onto Franklin Street and walk one block to Java Street. The **Astral Apartments (3)** are at 148 Franklin Street (1885, Lamb and Rich, architects). This apartment building was built as employee housing by Charles Pratt. Pratt owned the Astral Oil Refinery.

He joined John D. Rockefeller and seven others in forming the Standard Oil Company. He also founded Pratt Institute. The institute and his house are on the Clinton Hill walking tour in this guide.

Detour A: Just one block away, at 227 India Street, is the Bedi-Makky Art Foundry. The Iwo Jima Memorial statue was cast here.

Reverse your direction on Franklin Street. Walk past Kent Street and Greenpoint Avenue. Make a left on Milton Street. Walk the length of Milton Street. Most of the houses were built in the late 1800s. The **Greenpoint Reformed Church (4)** is on your right at #138. From 1867 to 1891 this was the home of the architect Thomas C. Smith who designed this and several other houses on this street. It then became the home to the church congregation that used to worship at what is now St. Elias, seen earlier on Kent Street.

Across the street is **St. John's Evangelical Lutheran Church (5)**: Theobald Engelhardt, architect. The Evangelische-Lutherische St. Johannes Kirche was built in 1891–1892 in the German Gothic style.

St. Anthony of Padua Church (6) (Roman Catholic) stands at the head of Milton Street on Manhattan Avenue. A Patrick Keely church, its 240-foot spire towers over Greenpoint. It was built in 1875.

Make a right on Manhattan Avenue. Walk past the freestanding **cast iron clock (7)** on the sidewalk in front of 753 Manhattan Avenue. Once a common sight on city streets, this is one of few remaining.

Ahead of you is Calyer Street. In the 1700s Jacobus Calyer's 65-acre farm was here. At the southwest corner of Manhattan and Calyer is the **Greenpoint Savings Bank (8)**. Built in 1908, its model and inspiration was the Pantheon, built in Rome in 27 B.C. by Marcus Agrippa. The architects here were Helmle and Huberty. The foundation is granite, the walls and columns are limestone, and the roof is slate.

Walk along Manhattan Avenue, Greenpoint's "Main Street," for four long blocks to Driggs Avenue. If you're hungry you may want to stop for pierogi along the way. Two favorites are the Polska Restaurant at 136 Greenpoint Avenue near Manhattan Avenue (718-389-8368) and the Polska Restaurant/Happy End Snack Shop at 924 Manhattan Avenue at the corner of Kent Street (718-389-8368). For lighter fare there's the Honeymoon Bakery and Sweet Shop at 837 Manhattan Avenue at Noble Street (718-389-5252) or the Piekarnia Rzeszowska at 948 Manhattan Avenue at the corner of Java Street (718-383-8142).

When you arrive at Driggs Avenue make a right. Driggs Avenue cuts through **McCarren Park (9)**. Both Edmund Driggs (d. 1891) and Patrick Henry McCarren (d. 1909) were Brooklyn politicians. As you walk down the avenue in the distance you'll see the onion domes of the **Russian Orthodox Cathedral of the Transfiguration of Our Lord (10)**. (No, you're not in St. Petersburg; this is still Brooklyn!) Begun in 1916, the cathedral took five years to build. Its architect was Louis Allmendinger. Inside, the icons mounted on the altar screen were painted by monks at the Monastery of the Caves, Kiev.

Retrace your steps on Driggs Avenue. Walk past Manhattan Avenue and continue on Driggs. On your right you'll see what remains of the arched pavilion entrance to the **McCarren Park Swimming Pool (11)**. The pool was opened in 1936, closed in 1984, and destroyed by fire in 1987.

Stay on Driggs Avenue. At Humbolt Street you'll see the massive **St. Stanislaus Kostka Church (12)**. It was built in 1890 and today has the largest Polish church congregation in the city. Both Pope John Paul II and Lech Walesa visited the church; two of the surrounding streets have been renamed for them.

Time for a rest? Take a few more paces on Driggs Avenue to **Monsignor McGolrick Park (13)**. The monsignor was a local pastor. Two items of note here: the shelter mimics those built in 18th-century France. It is a 1910 Helmle and Huberty design. The statue nearby is entitled "Monitor" and commemorates the Civil War ironclad ship built in Greenpoint. Antonio de Filippo modeled the Art Deco monument in 1939.

Your tour of Greenpoint ends here. The closest subway station is the Nassau Avenue stop (on the G line) at Nassau and Manhattan Avenues.

Index